A TIME
FOR
RISKING

MIRIAM ADENEY

A TIME
FOR
RISKING

PRIORITIES
FOR WOMEN

MULTNOMAH · PRESS
Portland, Oregon 97266

Special thanks to Mary Thompson—my "talking computer"—for her labor of love in typing this book, and to Lynne Baab for skillful editorial suggestions.

Unless otherwise marked, Scripture quotations are taken from the Holy Bible: New International Version, copyright 1973, 1978, 1984 by the International Bible Society. Used by permission of Zondervan Bible Publishers.

Scripture references marked LB are taken from The Living Bible, copyright 1971 by Tyndale House Publishers, Wheaton, Ill. Used by permission.

Scripture references marked NEB are from The New English Bible, © The Delegates of the Oxford University Press and the Syndics of the Cambridge University Press 1961, 1970. Reprinted by permission.

Scripture references marked NAS are from the New American Standard Bible, © The Lockman Foundation 1960, 1962, 1963, 1968, 1971, 1972, 1973, 1975, 1977. Used by permission.

Scripture references marked KJV are from the King James Version of the Bible.

Edited by Liz Heaney and Deena Davis
Cover design by Bruce DeRoos

A TIME FOR RISKING
© 1987 by Multnomah Press
Portland, Oregon 97266

Multnomah Press is a ministry of Multnomah School of the Bible, 8435 NE Glisan Street, Portland, Oregon 97220

Printed in the United States of America

Library of Congress Cataloging-in-Publication Data

Adeney, Miriam, 1945-
   A time for risking.

   Includes bibliographical references.
   1. Women—Religious life. 2. Women in Christianity.
I.Title.
BV4527.A32   1987   248.8'43   87-11299
ISBN 0-88070-192-7 (pbk.)

87 88 89 90 91 92 – 10 9 8 7 6 5 4 3 2 1

CONTENTS

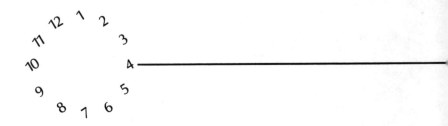

1

WHAT HAVE YOU COME TO THE KINGDOM FOR?

O nce there was a woman who lived in a harem.

But she was godly as well as glamorous. She didn't allow her situation to define the limits of her world view: She kept in touch with ordinary family living outside the harem. This wasn't through her parents, who were dead, but through a cousin. Every day he stopped by the back door of the harem to ask if she was okay. Here we have family loyalty under duress.

The time came when Esther's people, the Jews, were scheduled for extermination.

One evening her cousin said to her, "Maybe you've come to the kingdom for a time like this" (Esther 4:14).

As we know, Esther dared to be assertive. By astute planning, at the risk of her life, she got the genocide order reversed. Every year since then, Jews have celebrated the feast of Purim in honor of this strong, good woman who lived in a harem.

"Maybe you have come to the kingdom for a time like this." Today we are supposed to pour out our energies for Christ and his kingdom, that his kingdom may come, that God's will may be done. In light of this, we need to evaluate ourselves. Esther was conscious of what *she* had come to the kingdom for. Ask yourself, What have *I* come to the kingdom for? What gifts, friendships, dreams do I have that are unique? What will not get done in this world unless I do it (besides scrubbing my kitchen table)?

"Maybe you have come to the kingdom for a time like this," Esther's cousin said. Because of that, she stepped out. She blackened her eyelids with kohl. She rubbed gooey green henna paste into her hair to give it rich red highlights, and painted henna on her fingernails. She steeped herself in bath oils. Then she invited her husband, the king, to an intimate gourmet dinner, along with his chief advisor, Haman, the architect of genocide.

Here Esther put herself on the line: "I am a Jewess."

Would the king toss her on the garbage dump along with the rest of her disposable race?

Although Esther was in the good graces of the king and at the height of her powers, her position was precarious. Many of her fellow-wives saw the king for one night, then were banished into the harem never to talk to him again. Esther's predecessor, the high queen Vashti, had been shoved out because she had stood up for her convictions. Until this time Esther had been careful not to reveal her race to her husband.

Now she spoke up: "I am a Jewess."

Esther was where she was because she was beautiful. However, few beautiful women would have done what Esther did.

We study her not for what she had, but for what she did with what she had.

Esther employed everything at her disposal: sight, smell, taste, texture, timing . . . pitiful resources, really. She employed everything she had in the service of needy people to the glory of God. In so doing, she risked all her security and her future.

We may not be beautiful. But we all have some gifts and opportunities. What are we doing with them?

WHAT HAVE YOU COME TO THE KINGOM FOR?

When I became a mother I had to wrestle with this question.

My first baby didn't move out naturally. He was induced. It was traumatic. Lying on the examining table during my weekly check-up, I was looking forward to a cozy lunch downtown with my husband, Michael. Then we were going to the printer's to pick out paper for our baby announcement.

Suddenly my doctor looked up and broke rudely into my thoughts. "Your amniotic fluid is leaking," he exclaimed. "We'll have to induce this baby today. You go straight into the hospital."

I couldn't face it. I sneaked off to our restaurant rendezvous where I sat in a cold sweat, outraged with myself that I had to blink back tears and sniffles while people at other tables chatted as though nothing earthshaking was going on.

I'd had my labor all planned. I was going to walk around doing light chores, dipping into a new Doonesbury comic book. There were last-minute touches I had to give the house . . .

But those were surface objections. Deeper down, suddenly I was frozen rigid. My carefree days were over, I suspected. Never would I be independent again. For the next twenty years I would have to be responsible to another person, like it or not. I wasn't ready!

My Ph.D. program was half through. My part-time anthropology teaching job was anything but a secure career position. We had been able to spend only $20 on our sofa, only $200 on our car, and it didn't look like finances were going to improve. Would a baby trap me in this halfway state? Would I be able to grow as a person anymore? For eight years our marriage had been busy with travel and creative projects. Why in the world had we generated this new person to bring that lifestyle crashing down?

Now I have three children and have found them so revitalizing that I wish I had started sooner, so I would be young enough to have one more! But, sure enough, my fear when I went into labor was well-founded. Now I often wonder: Can I cope with anything more than today's crises?

I have only to wriggle out of my jeans and into a new wool suit, and baby is sure to make a mess all over it. The telephone rings. It's an important client three thousand miles away. Immediately my four-year-old son clamors, "Mom, does *D* start with red or yellow? Mom, is it *either* or *which?* Mom!" Baby swallows a deflated helium balloon. The four year old shoves his finger into a package of single-edge razors. Can I cope with more?

In spite of my own three-ring circus, I believe we women whether married or single—whatever our limiting circumstances—must continue to face the question: What have I come to the kingdom for?

I've described some of my constraints. What are yours?

Shyness?

A so-so education?

A non-Christian family background, so that you've lacked spiritual role models? Or a too-sheltered Christian family background, so that you have trouble making ordinary non-Christian friends?

A lack of confidence, so that you often find yourself on the fringe of the action instead of in the thick of it?

Money trouble?

A divorce?

A problem child?

A church structure that keeps you boxed in?

In spite of these liabilities, God intends great things for us and from us. He has rescued us from the kingdom of darkness and brought us into his kingdom. Why? Like Esther, we must ask: What have I come to the kingdom for?

WHAT IS THE KINGDOM?

The kingdom of God is a mystery. In one sense it exists in the future. When Christ reigns there will be no need of the sun because the Lamb-King will give off dazzling light. The wolf will lie down with the lamb. The trees of the field will clap their hands. And the earth will be filled with the knowledge of God like water fills the sea.

In one sense the kingdom exists in the future. But in another sense it is present here and now. Jesus said, " . . . if I drive out demons by the Spirit of God, then the kingdom of God has come upon you" (Matthew 12:28); "Heal the sick . . . and tell them, 'The kingdom of God is near you'" (Luke 10:9).

What is the kingdom? At bottom it is the rule, the reign, the sovereignty of God. George Ladd explains:

> Jesus said that we must "receive the kingdom of God" as little children (Mark 10:15). What is received? The Church? Heaven? What is received is God's rule. In order to enter the future realm of the Kingdom, one must submit himself in perfect trust to God's rule here and now.
>
> We must also "seek first his kingdom and his righteousness" (Matthew 6:33). What is the object of our quest? The Church? Heaven? No; we are to seek God's righteousness—His sway, His rule, His reign in our lives.
>
> When we pray "Thy kingdom come," are we praying for heaven to come to earth? In a sense . . . but heaven is an object of desire only because the reign

of God is to be more perfectly realized than it is
now. . . . Therefore, what we pray for is, "Thy kingdom come; *thy will be done* on earth as it is in heaven"
. . . in my church, as it is in heaven . . . in my life,
as it is in heaven.[1]

The kingdom means God's rule. God's reign over nature
because he created and maintains it. God's rule over people,
because he has created us and also because he redeems and
reconciles us. Working for the kingdom, then, means expressing, reiterating, claiming, insisting on that reign for our homes
and neighborhoods all the way up through our country's international relations.

Given this high-level job, how small are our ambitions.
How trivial are our pursuits. What have we come to the kingdom for? Shopping malls? Food processors? Home computers?
Luncheons? The command is to seek first the kingdom. Then
all these things may be added to us.

TAKING RESPONSIBILITY FOR OUR WORLD

Jewish women like Esther have a reputation for reaching
out to community problems. They have a heritage of taking
responsibility for their world because God has commissioned
them to do so—whether today they acknowledge him or not.
Consider this: In her prayer known as the "Magnificat," Mary
talks about how God will lift up the poor and punish the
oppressors:

My soul glorifies the Lord
and my spirit rejoices in God my Savior,
for he has been mindful
of the humble state of his servant.
From now on all generations will call
me blessed,
for the Mighty One has done great
things for me—
holy is his name.

His mercy extends to those who fear him,
from generation to generation.
He has performed mighty deeds with his arm;
he has scattered those who are proud
in their inmost thoughts.
He has brought down rulers from their thrones
but has lifted up the humble.

He has filled the hungry with good things
but has sent the rich away empty.
He has helped his servant Israel,
remembering to be merciful
to Abraham and his descendants forever,
even as he said to our fathers (Luke 1:46-55).

Mary's prayer is not unusual, however. It might have been almost any Jewish mother's prayer. Centuries before, when Hannah prayed for Samuel, she spoke about God's care for the down-and-outers and his judgment of their exploiters. She began with words that have a clear echo in Mary's song:

My heart rejoices in the LORD;
in the LORD my horn is lifted high.

Hannah revels in the mighty power of God, then explores how God applies his power:

The bows of the warriors are broken,
but those who stumbled are armed with strength.
Those who were full hire themselves out for food,
but those who were hungry hunger no more. . . .
[The Lord] raises the poor from the dust
and lifts the needy from the ash heap;
he seats them with princes
and has them inherit a throne of honor
(1 Samuel 2:1, 4, 5, 8).

When we pray for our children, as Mary did for Jesus and Hannah did for Samuel, do we also naturally bring to mind concern for the problems of our community and even of our international scene? If not, we need to refocus our priorities. We need to take more pride in our calling and to expand our vision.

Check yourself: What questions clutch you? What preoccupations weigh you down? What keeps you awake at night? Can you shift your thoughts to focus more on God's reign in each part of your personal world?

In this book I will argue that women should be involved in this world actively, assertively, sacrificially, and redemptively for two reasons: (1) because God has made us creative and commissioned us to exercise dominion on earth; (2) because God loves this world and constrains us to be his ambassadors of reconciliation. These are known classically as the "two mandates," the cultural mandate and the evangelism mandate. I have taken the liberty of calling them the creation mandate and the love mandate.

Frankly, these two callings are monumental. Once we glimpse their dimensions, we may gulp. At that point we must grasp hold of practical disciplines: How do we assess which activities we should be doing? How do we simplify our schedules? But the negative is not enough: How do we rekindle our enthusiasm at God's fire? By the positive disciplines of Bible study and prayer. Again and again we need encouragement to carve out time for these disciplines. We need to "exhort one another daily," to "speak often one to another" about warming up for these exercises.

No one needs this more than mothers. Motherhood adds multiple ripples and crosscurrents to the whirlpools of our lives. Delights engulf us. Demands swamp us. In this maelstrom, how do we make kingdom choices? Are there inside tips? How do we raise children so that they think in terms of priorities of the kingdom? In other words, are there ways to be Esthers for our families?

In this book we will explore what these mandates mean for women here and now. We will also get inspiration from other women scattered across time and space. Esther, for example, is one of our foremothers. Viewing her life, we learn a little more what it is to know God. We discover a little more

14

how God interacted with people. As we see how Esther served her generation according to the will of God, so our imagination is aroused to see how we might serve ours. Esther is part of our reference group, our heritage, our roots.

Because I am an anthropologist, I also want to learn from sisters in Christ in other cultures. What are their fears and dreams, their frustrations and delights? How are they developing their patch of God's world? How do they show love? There are many books on the market that give us an American perspective on being a Christian woman. But in this book we want to reach a little further.

1. George Ladd, *The Gospel of the Kingdom* (Grand Rapids, Mich.: Eerdmans, 1954), pp. 21-23.

2

WOMEN EXERCISE DOMINION

The Creation Mandate

When God made the earth, He could have finished it. But He didn't. He left it as a raw material—to tease us, to tantalize us, to set us thinking and experimenting and risking and adventuring. And therein we find our supreme interest in living.

He gave us the challenge of raw materials, not the satisfaction of perfect, finished things.

He left the music unsung and the dramas unplayed.

He left the poetry undreamed, in order that men and women might not become bored, but engaged in stimulating, exciting, creative activities that keep them thinking, working, experimenting, and experiencing all the joys and durable satisfactions of achievements. [1]

Who am I? What are my areas of creativity? Is there some aspect of "subduing the earth" that gives me holy joy in the doing of it? Some activity in which I lose myself? In which I express my unique creativity?

Can I expand this and make it a channel for loving my neighbors on a larger scale?

In Genesis 1:28 God commissions human beings with the creation mandate when he charges us to subdue the earth and have dominion over it. Earlier, in the preceding verse, God speaks of making people in "his own image, in the image of God." The two ideas—dominion and image-bearing—are connected. What does it mean to be in God's image? God is Creator. In his image, we are creative. So in his image, exercising our God-given creativity, we order and structure and develop and beautify his world—we exercise dominion. We shape raw material. We dream poetry. We struggle to achieve. God forbid that we bury his gift of creativity.

To do this, to exercise dominion, we need to identify our gifts and opportunities.

BEFRIENDING MOTHERS IN CRISIS

Laura Glessner models how one woman does it. By training, Laura is a special education teacher. Tom, her husband, is an attorney. They have two preschoolers, Joshua and SaraLynn Joy. Obviously, Laura has a number of options open to her. She's chosen to spend her time organizing pregnancy counseling centers because that is a big need in our society. Women who are horrified to find that they are pregnant have very little encouragement here to carry their babies to term. Yet many who abort regret it. One young girl wrote this letter to an anti-abortion advocate:

Dear Sir,

I agree with you 100% on abortion, but I had one. It was the hardest thing I ever had to do in my life. . . . My boyfriend and I fell in love, we made love, and I got pregnant. . . . My mom had noticed I had skipped my period. I was taken to the doctor. He said I was about six weeks pregnant. So she said I had to have an abortion. I had a counselor at Planned Parenthood who talked to me. She said my baby would never be adopted. Who was I to turn to? . . .

Would you mind telling me what you would have done? I didn't have a place to go, no money. Would you have taken me into your home? Paid my doctor bills and expenses?

My abortion is something I wish I had never done. I can remember looking at the doctor when it was done and saw him putting my baby in a plastic bag and then throwing it away in a garbage bag. Do you know how that feels? . . . If I had a place to go and people who cared about my baby and me, maybe my baby would be born and alive. It was supposed to have been born this month.

You're hurting girls that wanted their babies but didn't have any alternative.[2]

Laura's centers respond to that cry. They offer:

free pregnancy testing
education on pregnancy, abortion, and alternatives
housing with Christian families for clients who need
    temporary accommodations
childbirth classes
prenatal vitamins
clothing and furnishings to accommodate both
    mother and baby
classes for single parents
information on breastfeeding

> referrals for adoption or foster care
> referrals for medical care, legal assistance, or
> other needed community services
> ongoing friendship
> spiritual counseling regarding the Lord Jesus Christ
> guidance for schooling, jobs, goal-setting

Laura's centers are part of a spiraling network. In 1980 two such agencies existed in the U.S. By 1986, there were well over 300 nationwide. The busiest serve 200 women a day. About half the clients come in opposed to abortion personally, but many of them are under a great deal of pressure to abort. Because of the emotional stress they're under their opinions are volatile and changing. After counseling, however, 80 percent of those who are pregnant eventually have their babies.

Even rape victims sometimes decide to give their babies life. Ethel Waters, the famous Black singer, was a child conceived by rape. Her mother was twelve years old. In spite of pressure to abort, Ethel's mother birthed her and raised her. For such courageous, lonely women and girls, Laura Glessner's centers offer the support services, formal and informal, they need so desperately.

Some of the new little people who emerge are adopted into formerly childless families, meeting great needs. Laura's network is careful, though, not to encourage a woman to carry a child just so the center can provide a baby for someone else. Even reluctant mothers are not machines. They and their babies are made in the image of God, persons of dignity. The centers treat them that way.

Networks of friendly people need to surround such programs. Mothers may need caring homes before their babies are born. They may need community events and church fellowships where they are treated as ordinary people. After giving birth, young mothers who keep their children, whether married or not, need listening ears, shoulders to cry on, prayer over the telephone, weekends away, etc. Women who might be intimidated by Laura's administrative load can still give baby and maternity clothes and equipment. Others give their time.

Christians who oppose abortion must take it upon themselves to offer these services. Laura helps church people see this and then figure out how to do it.

God has commissioned us to "subdue the earth" and "have dominion over it." Laura knows she is called to exercise dominion in the society around her, to point to God's reign over day-to-day affairs. So she has considered her gifts and opportunities and set her priorities. Because of her, babies live. Women rediscover their preciousness. Their physical needs are met. They find friends. Some meet Christ. Couples' relationships are rekindled. Childless people receive children.

Laura has found an outlet for her creativity. She has identified her gifts and an opportunity to use them to bless God's world.

Have you?

HAVE YOU WATCHED GOD'S MOBILES SWAY?

"Subdue the earth and have dominion over it."
Well, what in the world could I subdue? you ponder. The lawn needs mowing. The kitchen needs repainting. Is that what God means?

Yes, that's part of it. Taking responsibility for your immediate physical environment. Tackling the mundane, the routine, the tyranny of the trivial. Beyond that, however, subduing the earth and having dominion means developing your personal creative expressions: handcrafts, music, gardening, entertaining, sports, conversation.

God is creative. He was the first sculptor. He designed the wind. "Have you considered his mobiles?" Edith Schaeffer asks in *Hidden Art.* "How about his light shows? And think about sound: God created both sound and ears."[3] He shaped comets and molecules, smells and colors.

Why bother with color? The first poem I wrote, around age twelve, wrestled with that: Why didn't God make do with black and white?

Color has its uses. It also has its beauties. And God delights in beauty. Snowflakes, seashores, and small children show us that. As the poet Keats once observed,

A thing of beauty is a joy forever:
Its loveliness increases; it will never
Pass into nothingness; but still will keep
A bower quiet for us, and a sleep
Full of sweet dreams, and health, and quiet breathing.
Therefore, on every morrow, are we wreathing
A flowery band to bind us to the earth,
Spite of despondence, . . . yes, in spite of all,
Some shape of beauty moves away the pall
From our dark spirits.[4]

Beauty and form matter. God evidently thought so when he made the world. And when he made me, he endowed me with creativity so that I, too, could struggle to shape patterns out of chaos.

From a practical point of view, unless I express my God-bestowed gifts, I am likely to feel irrelevant. Majoring in minors, it's easy for us women to become hypochondriacs, to go through our days mildly depressed. Kari Malcolm tells about this. The child of Norwegian missionaries, Kari grew up in China. In her book *Women at the Crossroads,* she describes how her parents took turns caring for their four children. They believed both mother and father had pivotal ministries.

Years later, when Kari was hiding passively behind her husband's ministry—because she thought that was what a good American Christian wife was supposed to do—and yet was feeling run-down and depressed, her mother scolded, "Of course. What do you expect?"

Kari explains, "My mother thought I should be out of the house, evangelizing the world and using all my God-given gifts to help others. As a nurse and a Christian, she believed very strongly that if we are not doing what God intends us to be doing, we will get sick."[5]

Kari followed her mother's advice. Today she and her husband both have vigorous service ministries.

In *Prescription for a Tired Housewife* psychologist James Dobson has observed that many women are bored because, among other things, they cultivate fewer interesting diverse interests than men. Men work on challenging projects while women do the same old laundry. These women need more than breaks; they need vocations—even part-time ones—in which they use their skills and gifts to accomplish something specific.

Ideally we can find ways to express our gifts through our jobs, whether in or out of the home. Although all jobs have their boring parts, even an apparently dull job may offer surprising scope for creative exercise of your particular strengths.

What are *you* gifted and called to do? That's your work. Can you do it in and around your job? If so, how blessed you are.

On the other hand, are you employed at something—for money, for professional satisfaction—that is good, but not best in light of the skills and opportunities God has laid on you? Should you modify your job so as to express your gifts more? Or do you even need to quit your job in order to get on with your true work?

Dorothy Sayers was a writer in England in the 1930s and 1940s. She was a Christian and a friend of C.S. Lewis. Her specialty? Detective stories. Her "Lord Peter Wimsey" mysteries continue to be excellent sellers today. Though her subject may have seemed frivolous, Dorothy took her work seriously. Her non-fiction book, *The Mind of the Maker*—a classic still read by Christian artists—describes the connections between God's creativity and human creativity, and how this is expressed in our work. For Dorothy, even detective stories should be written to the glory of God. The important thing was to learn what kinds of creativity God had gifted you with, she felt, and then to get busy using it. Because God has empowered us, our work is serious, whatever it is. We are not jacks-of-all-trades-and-masters-of-none. That's a trap we women easily can fall into.

Our diffuse responsibilities can water down our focus. For me, the years can become a blur of yellow-haired little boys, one after another. But we are *not* just general bundles of empathy, ready to serve any good cause. We are each uniquely and differently gifted. That's no light matter.

Such seriousness comes out in Mary McDermott Shideler's introduction to Dorothy Sayers' essay, "Why Work?":

> To be a person is to act, to work. In working we become our true selves and know ourselves and each other truly. Therefore work which is essentially trivial or shoddy, or consists of making things that are not worth making at all, diminishes the persons who engage in it at every level of production, exchange, and use. In contrast, they who love their work, and for love do it well, grow into the full measure of personhood. . . .
>
> The concept of work that Miss Sayers has proposed is neither puritanical nor medieval, but Christian. It grows from the belief that in work which is creative, human nature most nearly approaches its Creator. And for Miss Sayers, creativity is not restricted to the so-called creative arts. Building a house, typing a business letter, helping in the manufacture of well-designed and well-constructed objects for good purposes, teaching and healing and settling disputes and repairing machines are all creative functions when through those activities we participate in the processes which create and sustain societies and persons. . . .
>
> But "to aim directly at serving the community is to falsify the work; the only way to serve the community is to forget the community and serve the work. . . . If your heart is not wholly in the work, the work will not be good—and work that is not good serves neither God nor the community; it only serves Mammon." We are known by our work, as God is known by His.[6]

Listen to God's still, small voice. What are you gifted and called to do in this needy world? That's your work.

DOMINION IS MORE THAN DOING CRAFTS

But all we've considered so far is just the tip of the iceberg as far as subduing the earth is concerned. Arrested here, my vision remains far too small. I must lift my eyes, expand my horizons, and raise my consciousness regarding my larger neighborhood.

Subduing means taking responsibility for routine matters, yes.

Subduing means expressing my creativity, yes.

Subduing also means service to God's world.

We American Christian women are barely dipping our toes into this third area. We are scarcely touching the possibilities for significant service that surround us today. So the rest of this book will tend to focus on service.

In Darien Cooper's book, *You Can Be the Wife of a Happy Husband*—which has many biblical and useful ideas—she presents a wheel entitled "The Balanced Activities of the Wife." These include: husband, homemaking, children, appearance, money and security, in-laws, and outside activities. Cooper has an entire section on personal beauty tips. She advises the mother to try a new menu each week, even if her family does not like new things.

All well and good. But are these all the things that matter? We flip on the TV in the evening. South Africa is in political turmoil. Lebanon is exploding: orphans, medical needs, infrastructure destroyed, spiritual openness in pockets, physical hunger. Mexico's economy is in shambles: more desperate wetbacks cross the Rio Grande every week. Worldwide there is the overarching threat of nuclear disaster.

In our own city there are school problems, health problems, moral problems, political problems, abused children, lonely Indochinese and East Asians and Muslims. On our own street there are families breaking up. At work there are colleagues in crisis.

Everywhere there is a famine for hearing the Word of the Lord.

Certainly God has gifted some of us to be cooks, and some to be decorators. But he has called *all of us* to exercise dominion in his world. God is Creator of the Lebanese. He is Redeemer of the Mexicans. He is Lawgiver to the people of South Africa. He is Reconciler for the broken marriages in our office. He is Conqueror of the powers of darkness, those that would misuse nuclear power, and those that would abuse children. We women are called first to be ambassadors of this good news, not called first to aerobics. In this interdependent world, we can pour out our energies for missionaries in Lebanon and for the single mother down the street who needs a friend to laugh and cry with as she tries her hand at basic plumbing, wiring, and mechanics. We are called to express dominion in God's world through service to the needs around us.

Each of us can serve in a way that expresses our gifts.

LET THE BEAUTY OF GOD BE UPON US

Who am I? What are my areas of creativity?

> God tells us who we are. He tells us we are unique in the universe. Psalm 139 says he knows our "downsitting and uprising."
>
> It says that he knew me before my birth. Before I was a person, before I gave my first birth cry, God knew me, saw me and was aware of me.[7]

Sarah Gudschinsky said that. Ph.D., internationally known pioneer linguist and Bible translator, she was giving a chapel talk. She continued:

> Who am I? Well, I like to read *Scientific American*. I find articles on astronomy fascinating. Within my lifetime astronomers have learned that the stars we

26

see at night are only from one galaxy out of many galaxies. And our largest telescopes tell us there are billions of galaxies. And every one of those galaxies can have a billion stars. How many of those stars have solar systems like ours? Our earth is less than a speck of dust in the total of God's creation.

How can I think of the infiniteness of God? My mind can't take it all in. I run out of words.

And yet, out of the billions and billions of objects and time-years in the universe, there is only one fifth child of Ursula E. MacFarlane and Edward E. Gudschinsky, one named Sarah Caroline Gudschinsky. I am unique in the universe. You are unique in the universe. In all those billions of years, there never was another you and in all the time to come, there will never be another you. You are made by God into a pattern He will never repeat again.

Why on earth, then, am I worried about how I can be somebody? I *am* somebody, a unique creation of God.[8]

A few months before she died of cancer, Sarah said:

Do I need to worry about my life work? The choice is simple: I should be doing the will of God, what He prepared me for and what He put me on earth for.

God has a slot in his total eternal plan for each of us. That slot is exactly the shape of our heritage, experience and life, and He expects us to fill it. . . .

My responsibility is not to seek praise, but to be what God made me, unique in the universe; to do today with the whole of my strength what God has given me to do. And let the praise and status and the rest of it worry about itself.

A person who wants to be something different than God's purpose for him is like a cancer cell. That's what happened in my body. One kind of cell was not willing to stay where it belonged but wanted to fill up other space, crowding other cells out. We become cancer cells in the body of Christ when we want to be everything but what God wants us to be. . . .

If we become carbon copies of each other, then only a tiny, tiny bit of the glory of God would be visible. . . .

You and I—each one of us, individually—are unique in the universe, filling a spot that nobody else can possibly fill. If we don't do a job, others may "fill in," but they don't do what we would have done. They'll do something else: because they are uniquely different.[9]

Who am I?

Esther was creative. Laura Glessner. Sarah Gudschinsky. Each was gifted individually.

And so am I.

God has made me in his image. He has pursued and surrounded me with his grace so that I dare to speak up and affirm my uniqueness. He has commissioned me to pour my energies into some spot on his earth, to exercise dominion over his world. He cares about what I make.

One thing have I desired of the LORD, that will I seek after; that I may dwell in the house of the LORD all the days of my life, to behold the beauty of the LORD, and to inquire in his temple.

And let the beauty of the LORD our God be upon us: and establish thou the work of our hands. Yea, the work of our hands, establish thou it (Psalm 27:4; 90:17 KJV).

1. A. A. Stockdale, "God Left the Challenge in the Earth," *His* 25 (December 1964): 20.

2. Curt Young, *The Least of These* (Chicago: Moody Press, 1983), ix. Used by permission. The Crisis Pregnancy Centers are explicitly linked to the parent organization, the Christian Action Council. If you desire further information regarding the establishment, maintenance, and commitment required to set up such a Center, please write to: Christian Action Council, 701 W. Broad St., Suite 405, Falls Church, VA 22046.

3. Edith Schaeffer, *Hidden Art* (Wheaton, Ill.: Tyndale House, 1971), pp. 15-20.

4. John Keats, "Endymion," in *Masters of British Literature*, Vol. II, eds. Robert Pratt et. al. (Boston: Houghton Mifflin), p. 348.

5. Kari Malcolm, *Women at the Crossroads* (Downers Grove, Ill.: Inter-Varsity Press, 1982), pp. 35, 42.

6. Mary McDermott Shideler, Introduction to *Are Women Human?* by Dorothy Sayers (Grand Rapids: Eerdmans Publishing, 1971), pp. 14-15.

7. Sarah Gudschinsky, *Unique in God's Universe* (Dallas, Tex.: Summer Institute of Linguistics).

8. Ibid.

9. Ibid.

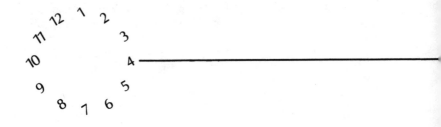

3

GOD'S WORLD

What Matters?

G ale Cincotta is a Chicago mother of six who is concerned about urban neighborhoods. She wants decent, affordable houses and services, and thriving local businesses for the people who live in the city.

She began learning about her community as a PTA mom. She never stopped: A few years ago she elicited a $175 million multi-bank loan for housing in poor neighborhoods. This changed some of the practices of banking across the nation. It also provided a model of community power that other neighborhoods can follow.

With six sons in Chicago public schools, Gale became aware that funding was distributed unfairly. Although she had no special training, she began speaking up, doing research, and organizing people regarding school funding. "If you have to run a family on very little money, you learn things," she says. "I don't have a college education, but I've figured out a budget and paid a mortgage. When you do these things, you learn to make connections. You imagine *you're* the board of education, with just so much money to spend, and you figure out how to spend it fairly."[1]

Before long, Gale was tackling wider community issues. She learned about "redlining." This occurs when bank planners draw a red line on maps around poor areas of the city. These areas become classified as poor credit risks. When this happens, homeowners and businesses there can't get loans. Naturally the neighborhoods deteriorate.

Gale confronted redlining by forming huge community coalitions; by picketing banks; by disrupting business by taking up officials' time opening new accounts, then closing them immediately; by putting up time-consuming legal challenges to the banks' lending records. These strategies brought bankers to the bargaining table to get her off their backs.

At the national level Gale spearheaded the successful lobbying which resulted in two pieces of federal legislation: the Community Reinvestment Act and the Home Mortgage Disclosure Act. These have become tools for pressuring local banks to extend loans in poor areas.

Just getting bankers to leave their paneled offices and tour poorer neighborhoods has brought satisfaction to Gale. As never before, some have seen that the poor are not just drug pushers, but also include responsible families. Some bankers have seen their city for the first time.

"When you start to look around your neighborhood and see what's really happening—people at the school board making decisions affecting your kids, realtors and bankers controlling your community—you come to a point where you either move out, or dig in and do something about the problem," Gale says.[2]

Seeing a need, Gale has reached out to serve. In so doing, she has exercised dominion. She has shown herself to be a faithful steward in her patch of God's world.

Gale is a model for us. As we have opportunities to affect our larger world, we must weigh them seriously. We dare not shrug them off simply because the situation is too complex for us to understand and we don't want to dirty our fingers. We can't throw out the excuse that we'll focus on the people we know and the needs we can get involved with personally.

True, one person can't do everything. In the next chapter we'll discuss how to sort through our activities and weed some out. Yet one person *can* try to grasp the outlines of the whole picture: her community's needs and its resources; the world's needs and its resources. Then she can pray intelligently. And then she can encourage others to serve where needed, and support them, rather than just duplicating what's already being done.

We American Christian women have remarkable opportunities. "Are you a slave? Don't let that worry you—but, of course, if you get a chance to be free, take it" (1 Corinthians 7:21 LB). We have a chance to influence many aspects of our world. Are we using our freedom?

WHAT ISSUES MATTER?

In our larger society we hardly need more electric shaving cream warmers. Or more verbal prostitutes peddling the products of the highest bidder. But some "subduing" is still essential. To face the coming energy crisis we need to achieve nuclear fusion. We need to penetrate inner space, to fathom the complex webs of a man's relations with himself and others. We need pioneers in leisure who will reawaken fantasy and festivals. On our TV channels we need script writers, cameramen, and producers who will live the holiness of Jesus Christ in the middle of a heady pagan whirl.

Thank God someone invented contraceptives. And contact lenses. And no-iron fabric. And Novocain. My dad, a doctor, remembers doing medicine before antibiotics were developed. Can you imagine that?

Yet, when Big Science tries to figure out what questions to answer, we need scientists who know why as well as how. Machines think, but people still ask the questions. Big Social Science supervises the manipulation of people through stimulus-response techniques toward certain goals. But which goals? Those who believe that people are innately corrupt as well as influenced by corrupt environments, who believe people are morally responsible to God and have the ability to make choices, will disagree with determinist colleagues over policies in education and in punishment and rehabilitation. We need people who will argue wisely and loudly enough to keep social scientists from building another system that doesn't fit God's design, another house on the sand that will come crashing down.

We need wide-awake, creative mothers and fathers who enjoy experimenting with chemistry in cooking and cleaning, and with physics and biology in the back yard. We need good neighbors. We need informed consumers. We need local and national politicians willing to push through a maze of lesser evils to sway our laws closer to God's standards. And in human development—in education, poverty programs, Native American affairs, counseling—those who follow the one who "went about doing good and healing all who were oppressed" should be right at the front of the line. We need evangelists to spread around the forgiveness and power of God, and Bible teachers to help others internalize the standards that will bring them into the most abundant life. And philosophers. "Where there is no vision, the people perish."

What do I know about our national health care options? The local school system? The state's economic picture—main agricultural and manufactured products, new job shifts? Parks and natural resources? Local programs for the poor? Recreational trends? The number of children in single parent families in my city? The sections of town where crimes are most frequent, and what those who live there think should be done about it?

What do I know about current world issues? In poorer countries that we pray for, many women need income-generating projects, according to the 1985 conference in Nairobi that climaxed the U.N. Decade for Women. Many also need family planning information transmitted through songs, video, and soap operas. Many need legal aid. Many want help regarding the health and education of their children. Many rural women in other countries need formal title to land which they lost when modern developers drew up titles and put them in men's names only. As more and more land is taken over by cash crops, women who grow the family's subsistence food in many countries find it harder to get enough land, titled or not. Or to get water. Urban women need equal pay, maternity leaves, childcare, and the option of flexible and reduced work hours if they have children. When we pray for poorer countries, we need to remember some of these issues.

Overall, what do I consider to be the biggest issues on the world's agenda? Beyond evangelism and nurturing people in godliness, Christian politician Stephen Monsma[3] lists these:

1. Possibility of nuclear holocaust
2. Need for stable economy
3. Poverty in the Third World
4. Increasing scarcity of fossil fuels
5. Racism

Would I agree that these are crucial? Am I directing any energy toward any of them? Even any regular prayer?

POWER IS NOT A DIRTY WORD

Confronting existing power structures is part of our call to dominion. Exercising dominion may mean setting up separate structures like pregnancy counseling centers as Laura Glessner does. More often, though, it calls for wading into established structures as Gale Cincotta does on behalf of urban neighborhoods. Often, the problems new organizations wipe up are spillovers nudged by imbalances in existing structures. We need to stem leaks at their source. To do that, we need to strengthen our power bases, like Laura and Gale do.

Power sometimes has been considered a dirty word. Power conflicts have been considered un-Christian. But these views are not quite accurate. God is a God of power, and we praise him for it. He commissions us to subdue the earth, to exercise dominion, and that requires power. We want power, not to lord it over anybody, but in order to serve efficiently.

"My wife belongs to the League of Women Voters and also to our church women's society," a man said in a recent discussion. "Both these organizations see evils that need to be corrected. Both hope to help. But the League of Women Voters arms itself with political techniques, with management techniques, and wades into the arena of power with carefully selected weapons. The church women's society just hosts discussions, passes internal resolutions, and writes papers."

He summed it up: "The League gets specific results; the church society doesn't."

This was not always so. Time was when women's church societies were a power to be reckoned with, especially in relation to missions. Today their power has waned, with sad side effects. In *All Loves Excelling* R. Pierce Beaver has traced the rise of women's mission committees in North America, beginning with the "Cent Society" in 1802. Over the years such societies took keen interest in the work and life of individual women missionaries. Each member of a society felt personally involved with the ministry on the field. Their concern and the publicity they generated enabled some single women missionaries to assert their gifts in ministry, rather than serving as girls-of-all-work for married couples. Missionary wives, too, received moral support.

Beyond a woman's focus, however, these societies maintained missions education and world awareness for the grass roots rank and file in the churches. When in mainline denomination after denomination the women's mission societies were co-opted and amalgamated into general mission boards, this lively grass roots missions education slipped down the agenda, and its momentum has never been regained.

Beaver states:

> The women's societies were successful because they
> gave women responsibility which nurtured Chris-
> tian character and enlisted vast numbers of them
> through auxiliaries in genuine involvement. . . .
> When direct participation, education, and promo-
> tion were taken from them and they were no longer
> asked to do the seemingly impossible, passionate
> devotion cooled. . . . Girls have not been 'brought
> up in the mission' as were their mothers and have
> not had the challenge of vocation held constantly
> before them.[4]

Commenting on the decline of interest in missions in mainline churches, Beaver says, "The author concludes that this
lack of concern and involvement is in large measure due to
the decline of women's direct participation."[5]

As God gives us opportunities, we should seek leadership
and power so that we can serve better.

This may mean we women will need to reorient our world
view slightly. Many of us tend to identify more with Christ in
his suffering than with Christ in his authority. Where this is
true, we need to stretch a little.

Consider this example. A few years ago, a seminary class
was studying Luke 4:18-19, which describes Jesus reading and
applying to himself the words of Isaiah.

> The Spirit of the Lord is on me,
> because he has anointed me
> to preach good news to the poor.
> He has sent me to proclaim freedom
>   for the prisoners
> and recovery of sight for the blind,
> to release the oppressed,
>   to proclaim the year of the Lord's
>   favor.

"What role in this passage do you identify with?" the seminarians were asked.

"The preacher," answered the white men in the class.

But not the women and minority men. Who did they identify with? "The poor, the prisoners, the blind, and the oppressed."[6]

Of course we are called to identify with Christ in his suffering. We are called to be poor. But we are also called to be Spirit-filled messengers. We women, as well as men, are called to power. Not self-centered power, but God-centered power. We are to subdue the earth and have dominion over it.

Power is not bad. It's a force, like electricity, cars, or computers. But neither is it good. That's the great delusion of many church and parachurch leaders. Such leaders need to pray like Moses, Solomon, Daniel, Nehemiah, and Paul, "Oh Lord, my group and I make such stupid mistakes. Forgive us. Discipline us. Help us turn around—again and again. Renew and recharge us. And let us walk beside you still."

But power is not bad.

Nor is confrontation. As power can be exercised lovingly, so confrontation can be engaged in graciously. And when we really care, we do confront people. If someone molests your child, you confront. If someone sells you a shoddy vacuum cleaner, you confront. Clearly for our own personal interest and convenience, we will confront people. How much more readily then should we be willing to do it for the kingdom of God and for the love of our neighbors?

We can serve God this way on a personal level as well as an institutional level.

John is a friend who has gifts in the area of conflict. His conflicts nurture people. An editor, he was developing a curriculum recently. One contributing Christian writer, earmarked for a top spot, turned out to be a loud mouth, show-off, and all-around pest. When Earl started to flirt with some of the married young women editors it was the last straw.

I would have been embarrassed, irritated, and angry. I would have washed my hands of him.

But not John.

He took Earl aside and in a slow drawl read him the riot act. He enumerated every offense Earl had committed during the project. He reiterated what dreams they had had for Earl. So evident was John's caring, even in the context of his anger, that Earl, the macho man, started to cry.

As they talked, Earl confided that he had never felt able to live up to his father's expectations. So he always felt he had to prove himself. That talk turned out to be the beginning of a change in Earl's life. The last time I stopped in John's office, Earl happened to call long distance.

"You know what?" he told John. "My work relations are better, my writing is better, even my family life is better."

As I sat and eavesdropped, John shared a new area of vulnerability that he had just entered—ice skating—and how insecure he felt as he took his first steps.

I have seen John enter into constructive and redemptive conflict with his boss when all the other workers around him just fumed and flailed.

Conflict is not un-Christian, whether it's interpersonal confrontation like John's or institutional confrontation like Gale Cincotta's. Confrontation may be an extension of dialogue. It may well mean caring.

For the sake of God's world, we women must develop thicker skins and cannier bargaining skills so that we can engage in conflicts more successfully. We are debtors not just to foremothers who have modeled pioneering but also to some who have modeled conflict. In Europe in the nineteenth century, women's rights were promoted by two major groups: humanists, through the French revolution, and evangelical Christians, through a series of reforms in England protecting women from gross exploitation. The first movement emphasized women's common equality with men. The second emphasized women's special needs, especially mothers' needs. Both emphases are necessary.[7] We owe something to those women who were willing to enter conflicts in order to pass on to us a better heritage.

I do not mean to champion Western activism. Sometimes God speaks not through fire but through a still, small voice. Sometimes we need to teach a Sunday school class of five girls. Would that there were more men who would teach a Sunday school class of five boys and would join us regularly in the quiet work of visiting the fatherless and widows. But as we have opportunity, we should break out of our trivial pursuits, give up our small ambitions, and think big.

ARE WOMEN RESPONSIBLE?

We women hesitate. Some of these areas seem almost outside our sphere. Until someone straightens out those confusing Pauline passages on women, we fear to usurp the prerogatives of men. Too often we fail to see that God has commissioned us, along with men, to exercise dominion on earth. We fail to see that the world and the church need our energies poured out. We fail to see that we are likely to be sick, or at least to suffer low-level depression, unless we express our God-given gifts. So we tiptoe around, oblivious to world events, stirring messes of pottage and letting our birthrights rot.

God has commissioned us along with men to subdue the earth and have dominion over it. "Eve was not created to cater to Adam's material needs or to produce his children. She was to be a 'helper corresponding to him' with a wider responsibility in creation," says Valerie Griffiths, lecturer in Old Testament at London Bible College and long-term missionary with her husband, Michael, in the Overseas Missionary Fellowship. Not all Christians have so interpreted Scripture, she notes.

> Calvin interpreted (woman as helpmeet) as meaning that a woman was 'a kind of appendage to the man,' owing her existence entirely to the necessity for supplying his needs. Clyde Narramore says, 'Woman was not made for herself, but to complete

the man.' This is another instance where the culture of the commentator prejudges the interpretation. The Hebrew word *helper* occurs twenty-one times in the Old Testament. Apart from its use twice here of the woman, four of these occurrences are general usages and the other fifteen are references to God as the 'helper' of his people; so it cannot in itself mean that the 'helper' is secondary and subordinate to the one helped. So far the only 'rule' mentioned is that of mankind over creation—not over each other. In their own relationship, mutual need and complementarity are clear. They are created to serve God together. . . . If men can recognize that when they operate without women, something is lacking, and if women can recognize that too often they shrug off God-given responsibilities out of a mistaken view of femininity, then we can begin to discover how God calls us to serve him together in today's world."[8]

We exercise dominion because God has commissioned us to do so. Also, we exercise dominion because the world and the church need our full energies.

The sad truth is that women pioneers—women on the fringes, such as missionary women—seem to accomplish more in relation to their immediate environment and to the men around them. When people are poor, women's productivity matters and is valued. But when people are rich and well-organized, women often are valued as decor or as property rather than as producers. They may have full and flurried schedules, but the activities are peripheral.

When an organization is stretching, every worker counts. But when an organization is consolidating, women become decorative assistants.

Should our churches be consolidating or stretching? If we take a good look at our world, if we even take a good look down our street, we will realize this is no time to be balanced. There are areas of our world today that desperately need pioneering—the slums of cities like Mexico, approaching thirty million people. There are areas nearby—the areas that spawn lots of unwed teenage mothers. There are professions and spheres of life that need Christians to show forth God's reign; these can be as scary as anything that pioneer women faced. This is a time for risking, pioneering, daring, for exercising our ingenuity with all our might.

If we were to recover a true sense of our poverty, women *and* men might see the urgency of being producers. If we saw that the needs are so great that the daughters *must* prophesy, men *and* women would spill over out of our church bureaucracies and new jobs and ministries would be created. In this effort the church needs every worker she's got. If we care for God's earth, for people, for his church, we dare not hang back on the fringes.

LOVE HURTS

"Whenever I think about refugees I get upset!" a woman once said to me. "I know God doesn't want me to be upset. So I've decided not to think about them any more."

Was Christ upset when he was on earth? Was the experience of the crucifixion upsetting? In a perfect world, in Eden, in heaven, upsets might not be necessary. But in this world, God troubles the comfortable so that we might comfort the troubled. When we are in trouble, when we are the refugees, we learn the value of this.

Of course we don't have all the answers. In one of his poems, my neighbor Ed Harkness describes himself late at night trying to write:

> I wish I could say, "Before me: hills pleated and Indian, a doddering barn spreading its one good wing of morning shadow, cottonwoods, wild irises, a chestnut mare chewing her singular vision of dusty grass." I long to say "Night, snow," long for sparks to whir from a stone chimney, become stars, flutter down as black blossoms, as tiny extinct wings.
>
> But no.

Only this clutch of clutter before me. Kids are down,
Linda drowses, exhausted, novel toppling off her
chest. I stay up to catch the late news: flies dance
in the nostrils of starved, haunted children, whose
eyes are vast moonscapes. Then the toothpaste ad,
the one that gives your breath a fresh, minty taste.
Then the eyes again. I hate them. I switch the channel and there they are, dying once more. I twist the
color adjustment till their reed-like arms burst into
bluegreen flames, then I flip off the whole mon-
strous world, sick, wanting to growl, retch.[9]

I don't have all the answers. Does that mean life is ultimately absurd? Should I look at things that are happening in
my society as any atheist would, or should I try to see the hand
of God in current events? Praying through the news energizes
me to exercise godly dominion in my patch of the earth as I
have opportunity.

Yet how easy it is to let go of dominion.

"How do we cultivate a walk with God?" asked a speaker
at a recent Christian women's conference I attended.

"Well, I don't watch TV much any more," she answered
her own question. "I don't even listen to the news or read the
paper. They filled my mind with too much garbage."

And yet this morning as I heard of a cholera breakout in
the wake of ten thousand deaths caused by a storm in
Bangladesh, I could struggle in prayer for those people while
I rinsed the breakfast dishes. As I heard of deadly soccer riots
in Britain, and of a murder in Seattle, I could lift up the
culprits and the bereaved families in prayer.

We don't have all the answers. There are paradoxes. There
are absurdities. There are problems too big for us. Yet un-
knowns add a tang to the life of faith. Through it all, God
never calls us to be ostriches. Without the complete printout,
we still are called to exercise dominion in God's world.

1. Ann Witte Garland, "Gale Cincotta," *Ms.*, January 1986, p. 50.
2. Ibid.
3. Stephen Monsma, *Pursuing Justice in a Sinful World* (Grand Rapids: Wm. B. Eerdmans, 1984), pp. 27-31.
4. R. Pierce Beaver, *All Loves Excelling: American Protestant Women in World Mission* (Grand Rapids, Mich.: Eerdmans, 1968), pp. 182, 200-203.
5. Ibid.
6. Justo and Catherine Gonzalez, *Liberation Preaching* (Nashville: Abingdon, 1980), pp. 77-78.
7. These two historical emphases—women as equal with men, and women in need of special benefits—are mirrored in the 1986 bombshell book *A Lesser Life: The Myth of Women's Liberation in America*. Sylvia Hewlett, a senior economist at the United Nations, is the author. Equality is not enough, she argues. Mothers have special needs. And a great many women are mothers at some point.
8. Valerie Griffiths, "Mankind: Male and Female," in *The Role of Women: When Christians Disagree*, ed. Shirley Lees (Leicester, UK: Inter-Varsity Press, 1984), pp. 72-95.
9. Edward Harkness, "Tonight," in *Fiddle Wrapped in a Gunny Sack* (Story, Wyoming: Dooryard Press, 1984). Used by permission.

4

SAYING NO

Priorities and Planning

Y ou're probably thinking: It makes me tired just to listen
to her!
Listen: I tumble into bed a zombie. I know what it is
to crumble up half an onion by hand and toss it into the fry
pan, bits of husk and all, because I have a baby on one shoulder
and can't manage a knife. I no longer play the violin, make
yogurt or bake bread, sew most of my clothes, write many
personal letters, or even talk much on the phone. My nonwork-
ing neighbors bowl, take fun classes, and work out at figure
salons; I don't have those luxuries. My childless colleagues

enjoy luncheons, parties, and pivotal committee meetings; I can't. That limits my decision-making power in the institutions where I teach. My yard has a very country look. Inevitably, when I'm pushing toward a deadline, one of my sons will shove a lima bean up his nose or a shampoo bottle down the toilet. And there are afternoons when I toss all priorities to the wind and sit down with a detective novel.

YOU CAN'T HAVE IT ALL

Of course we can't do it all.

None of us can. Singles are inundated with the whole gamut—plumbing and car mechanics as well as hostessing and beauty. Because I am a mother, though, it is a mother's overload that I know best.

Anne Morrow Lindbergh wrote about this:

> I understand why the saints were rarely married women. . . . I am convinced it has nothing inherently to do, as I once supposed, with chastity or children. It has to do primarily with distractions. . . . Woman's normal occupations run counter to creative life, or contemplative life or saintly life.[1]

Distractions. Catherine Booth (1829-1890), co-founder of the Salvation Army, was a tough lady. Yet even she was pummeled by distractions. When Catherine had four children, the eldest age four (and the prospect of possibly a dozen more), she began to preach. Frequently thereafter she addressed two or three thousand people—uneducated, disruptive people of the slums. After the meetings she counseled those who came forward; no big Billy Graham organization stood behind her to provide support personnel. So it was left to Catherine to find jobs for all the newly reformed prostitutes and pickpockets. For years to come she would correspond with them. Beyond this, whenever possible, Catherine made it her habit one evening a week to visit the families of alcoholics.

Catherine continued preaching right through eight children. When she traveled as an evangelist they often traveled with her. Then the guest speaker would arrive complete with children, nursery furniture, and also a big rug—so that her offspring would not ruin the carpets in the homes where she stayed.

She had one assistant, who was more like a sister than a servant, who stayed with the Booths all her life although rarely could they pay her. One helper for eight sets of diapers without any automatic washer or dryer in rainy England. Catherine and her assistant made all the children's clothes until the children were twelve years old. What kind of mother was she? Her letters to her children pulsate with the passionate, individual thought she gave to each child.

At the same time—without a word processor—she wrote eight books. (Fortunately she had done her Bible study early— she had read the entire Bible through eight times by the time she was thirteen.)

Catherine Booth understood that she was to have dominion. Usually she charged ahead decisively and enthusiastically. How poignant, then, are a few excerpts from her letters written when distractions threatened to tear her apart:

> While I was nursing my baby [at the breast], many a time I was thinking of what I was going to say next Sunday; and between times noted down with a pencil the thoughts as they struck me. . . . If I had only time to study and write I should not fear now, but I must be content to do what I can consistently with my home duties and leave the future to the Lord. . . . I continue my visitations among the [alcoholics]. . . . I can only devote one evening per week to it. . . . They said that I must prepare myself to preach at night very often. I told them it was easy talking, etc., they little knew what it cost me, nor anybody else either, except the Lord. You see I cannot get rid of the care and management of things at home, and this sadly interferes with the quiet necessary for preparation. . . . I shall not consent [to increase preaching]. I cannot give the time to preparation unless I could afford to put my sewing

out, and it never seems to occur to any of them that
I cannot do two things at once, or that I want *means*
[italics hers] to relieve me of one while I do the other.

Later, on the marriage of her gifted daughter Katie,
Catherine speaks with rare wistfulness:

Mothers will understand . . . a side of life to which
my child is yet a stranger. Having experienced the
weight of public work for twenty-six years, also the
weight of a large family continually hanging on my
heart, having striven very hard to fulfill the obligation on both sides, and having realized what a very
hard struggle it has been, the mother's heart in me
has shrunk in some measure from offering her up
to the same kind of warfare. . . . The consecration
which I made on the morning of her birth, and
consummated on the day that I gave her first to
public work, I have finished this morning in laying
her again on this altar.[2]

"What a very hard struggle it has been . . ." Catherine
revealed. What a hard struggle it is to be a responsible person.
How can we cope—particularly we mothers?

Beverly Sills, world famous opera singer, mother of a
handicapped daughter, vibrant friend—spoke of the struggle
when she gave a commencement address at Barnard College
a couple of years ago,

Women are told today they can have it all—career,
marriage, children. You need a total commitment
to make it work. Take a close look at your child. He
doesn't want you to be bright, talented, chic or
smart—any of those things. He just wants you to
love him. He will be the one who pays the price for
your wanting to have it all. Think carefully about
having that baby. Not to have it would be a great
loss. . . . To have it without a commitment to it would
be a great tragedy. There are two keys: one, believe
in yourself; two, love. You must ooze it from every

pore. Love your work, your husband and your child, not just to hear his needs but to feel his needs. For your husband you must reserve that 30th hour of the day when he has you all alone to himself. If you wonder when you'll get time to rest, well, you can sleep in your old age.[3]

To say we can't do it all, however, gives us no excuse to drop out of the battle altogether. God has commissioned us to exercise dominion and to love our neighbors. God has handed us multiple responsibilities. But in each area we must simplify. Because we can't do it all, because our resources are limited, the crucial question is: How do we slice our priorities?

How Do You Slice Your Time?

One tool is the word *no*.

No is a knife word. No job. No skills. No husband. No children. No entrance. No exit. No hope. Not here. Not home. Not done. Nobody. Nothing. Nowhere.

Yet we need it.

The ancient Chinese philosopher Mencius once said, "Before a man can do things, there must be things he will not do." How much more true this is for a woman.

How do we slice our priorities? When her husband took a job in agricultural research in the Philippines, Betty Mae Dyck was sure she could get by without a maid.

Of course I can do my own housework! she thought.

However, she says,

When I had lived in the Philippines for less than two weeks during the steaming rainy season, I began to think differently about household help. My energy level sank in the debilitating heat and humidity. Perspiration pouring from our sweat glands made two complete changes of clothing a day a social necessity.

51

The frozen and canned fruits and vegetables, mixes and other convenience foods I had relied on so heavily in Canada were unavailable in the Filipino market. Vegetables, fruits, meats, and eggs had to be bargained for—each item separately. Then one had to hurry home and wash everything carefully to prevent spoilage. It seemed one had to bargain for, wash, sort, peel and chop everything before any actual cooking took place. The process took its toll in emotional as well as physical energy.

My mildewy, dusty, insect-infested house soon depressed me. Especially so after I was invited to share a cup of coffee with a neighbor. I was met at the door by a smiling little maid, carrying a tray of neatly folded laundry, who then seated me politely and immediately called to her companion to bring snacks. She went to call her mistress. Soon another maid appeared bringing a perfectly laid tea tray. . . .

During those early weeks, it became clear that I couldn't manage to keep my house clean, let alone attractive, and my husband fed, doing everything alone. Even if I could do it alone, I already knew I would just barely manage. Not enough time would be left to keep myself properly groomed and dressed, and no time at all for a ministry to the people around me. That was frightening, discouraging, and disappointing.[4]

Betty Mae hired maids, struggled to discover rules for relating to them successfully, and then went on to teach in local public and Christian schools, to capitalize small handicraft businesses run by needy Christians, to conduct innumerable Bible studies, to do church work, to write books, and to counsel a continual flood of guests. Meanwhile, by hiring maids, she gave work to Filipinos and led several of them to Christ. To do that, to have this expanded ministry, she had to let others into her privacy. She had to share the control of her home.

Marjory Stewert is a college English instructor. She is also a writer. For years she has waded through mounds of essays into the wee hours of the morning. This year, however, she has decided, "I'm going to drill grammar rather than assign so many essays." The students will learn, and Marjory will have time to sleep, to enjoy, and to write.

Joy Agarra is an artist, musician, and all-around creative person. She and her husband plan to be missionaries to Mexico. For eight years he has been in college and graduate school. Money? Don't mention it. In order to keep her toddler with her, Joy works at a boring secretarial job near home rather than at a more challenging one downtown. She's no martyr, however. Instead of putting much of her paycheck into heat for their house, Joy has been designing and building a full-scale harp! On Saturdays, in spite of heavy work schedules, Joy and her husband have started the only Sunday school for mentally retarded adults in their city. Beyond that, once a week, Joy squeezes in a course in Gaelic language.

How does she slice her priorities? Not the way we would, perhaps. Yet they've enabled her to survive eight years of "student wifehood" with flair.

Professional writer Ellen Seton speaks for many when she admits, "Make no mistake—I don't have it all. No woman with children and a job can have it all—that's women's fib. What she can have is a little bit of a lot of things or a lot of a few things. What I have is a lot of time for my child and my work, only a little bit of time to be alone with my husband and almost no time for anything else."[5]

What's disappeared from Ellen Seton's life? Baths (replaced by showers). Crossword puzzles. Pets. Nail polishing. Sending birthday cards. Any cooking fancier than cheese sandwiches. Languorous, spontaneous love with her husband. Lunches with friends. Sometimes even Christmas cards. Weekend mornings in bed with the newspaper and coffee. Leisurely strolling arm in arm in the evening. Spur of the moment plans to slip away for the weekend.

Of course we can't do it all. Yet look at Betty Mae, Marjory, Joy, and Ellen. Look at Beverly Sills. Along with saying no to some things, they have said yes to other things, significant things.

DON'T ANSWER THE WRONG QUESTION

Sweet Suffering is a book by a sixty-eight-year-old psychiatrist, Natalie Shainess.[6] It aims to teach us women how to be more assertive. Among its recommendations: When someone asks you a question, don't feel you must answer. Don't feel limited to that topic. Follow the example of politicians. Answer briefly, then expand the topic to an area that interests you more.

Or when people have an agenda or plan, don't argue. But consider whether you should have different plans. If so, make them, and operate in terms of those.

For example, at a party someone asks you, "And what do you do?"

"I'm a homemaker," you smile. The conversation dwindles, and you feel resentful because your chosen job hasn't been given much respect.

But it's partly your fault. How does the stranger know you're committed to homemaking rather than having just gotten stuck in it? You must take the responsibility to channel the conversation in ways that will enable you to share yourself.

"And what do you do?"

"I'm a homemaker," you smile, "and I happen to be particularly interested in the development of children." Or, "and I put a lot of my energies into local school activities." Or whatever distinguishes you. Give your conversational partner a break, and a direction.

How like Jesus this sounds. When people asked him questions, he often turned the questions around and led the discussion to something quite different. People continually struggled to fit him into their plans. Yet how often he slipped away.

In Mark 1:37-39, for example, Peter hustles up: "Your public is calling! You must come!"

Jesus shrugs, "I have another agenda." And he walks away. Jesus knew how to say no—in order to say yes.

Women traditionally have been more adaptive than assertive. We have fit in more than we have spoken up. We have served more than we have taken charge. We have nurtured domestic cocoons more than we have confronted world powers.

Adapting, fitting in, serving, and nurturing are beautiful. We don't want to give up those roles.

But we need to balance between being adaptive and being assertive. Between serving others' priorities and obeying our own vision.

Fundamentally, of course, our focus is neither others' priorities nor our own, but the priorities of the kingdom of Christ. In practice we don't always agree what the priorities of the kingdom are. So we must give space to those with whom we disagree. We must treat them with respect. Nevertheless, we must return again and again to Jesus' pithy reminder that if we seek first his kingdom and his righteousness, all our various activities will find their rightful niche.

KINGDOM PRIORITES

Try this: Lay out a large sheet of butcher paper or construction paper, take up a few colored marking pens, and draw a picture of your life (as you'd like it to be) five years from now. Stick figures are fine: this is for your eyes only. Cover as many aspects of your life as you can: friends and family, career, intellectual growth, spiritual growth, finances, service activities, hobbies and skills, fun flings. Include your wild dreams. This exercise will help you make contact with some of your unconscious hopes.

From this picture select a list of goals to work toward this year. You might break some of these down into steps, with deadlines. For example: "I will greet one stranger and try to start a conversation every week, starting this week."

Before you get too committed though, you need to step back and ask yourself: Are these worthy goals? I use two tools here, one for critiquing my goals, and one for arranging them in a hierarchy according to importance.

Saying No

To critique my intended activities I ask these questions:

How important is it? How much power does it have
to affect the world?
How needy is it?
Can or will anyone else do it, or am I uniquely fitted
to do it by gifts or by being on the spot?
Is it new? Does it break ground? Or is it something I
have done before? Will I grow?
Is this an obligation because of loyalty to an
institution? (Like wiping the kitchen table?!)
What is the financial compensation?
Are my time and energy already committed?

Next, I arrange my goals in order of importance. A year
ago, using the criteria above, I divided my current projects
into three lists:

1. Top priority
2. Fairly important
3. Interesting but not crucial

To my surprise, most of my planned activities fell into lists
2 and 3. In list 1 were specific needs in my relationship with
God, specific spiritual and relational needs of my children and
my husband, needy friends outside my comfortable network,
and creative writing that nobody was urging me to do. These
lists helped me discover where I had priorities without plans.
Now, one year later, I can thank these lists for pushing me to
take specific steps in priority areas that I would have let slip
by otherwise.

For you, kingdom priorities might mean saying no to talking on the telephone so much. Or saying no to well- established
committees in order to serve on other more needy committees.
Saying no to certain kinds of reading in order to do other,
more crucial reading. Saying no to thinking so much about
how you feel or about the way you look—saying no to your
"pity parties." Kingdom priorities might mean monitoring
your imagination—"casting down imaginations, and every
high thing that exalteth itself . . . and bringing into captivity

every thought to the obedience of Christ" (2 Corinthians 10:5 KJV). It might mean limiting the time you spend thinking about fashion, shopping, romance, eating out, backpacking, gardening, skiing, soap operas, novels, gossip, or whatever catches your imagination, in order consciously to focus a certain amount of your thoughts on people's need for Jesus, on world hunger, on nuclear weapon dangers, on teenage mothers. Kingdom priorities might mean saying no to spending so much time with certain friends in order to spend time with other friends who need you more. Or limiting your mindless conversations, in order consciously to make your conversations channels of grace.

There's a time for frivolous activities. They shouldn't be scratched out of your agenda because they're "not important." We need to dare to act out some of our silly dreams. On the other hand, our dreams deserve some scrutiny. Some will prove to be hollow. Others will be seen to be redundant. When I first drew a picture of Miriam-five-years-from-now, I included a sketch of myself traveling in Africa. Later, when I looked at my goals in light of God's kingdom, realizing that he has given me a good deal of ministry in Asia and Latin America, I saw that it's probably not necessary for me to go to Africa too. Struggling toward that is probably just greed. When I realized that, I was able to loosen my grasp on that goal. If God sends me to Africa, well and good. If not, that's one thing I probably don't need. Nor does God's world.

So make time to dream without inhibitions. Then, later, critique those dreams.

Here are a few more questions:

> What will I do this week that I haven't done before?
> Who do I want to relate to this week?
> What am I struggling with?
> What am I hoping for?
> What am I learning?

On weeks when I need a pep talk, I use these. Scanning the week ahead, I ask myself these questions before I plan my

Tips for Efficient Housekeeping

Physical Sorting

- For temporary, one-minute cleanups, sweep toys to the side of the room.
- Use large garbage bags (or cardboard boxes), labeled, to store stuff of the same category that you don't have time to sort through right now—files from a certain project; Christmas decor; your youngest child's outgrown clothes.
- Give each child one special cup, and use that cup all day long.
- Sometime when you go to visit a friend, ask her if you can bring along a kitchen drawer that needs sorting out. She can pull out one of hers, and you can have a drawer-sorting chat.

Routine Jobs

- Let everyone above age ten put away his/her own laundry. Store a separate box or basket for each near the dryer. For "hangables," mount hooks near the dryer.
- Discover which simple meals your family likes, and stick to those except for special occasions.
- Discover which meals some family member likes enough to cook himself/herself. My eight-year-old boy, for example, will do nearly an entire taco salad meal joyfully.
- Regularly try these simple and low-cost meals:

      -Cheese, bread, fruit
      -Fresh green salad—cheese, eggs, nuts, cold
       meats are optional additions—and bread
      -Soup and bread, with special jam or honey
      -Scrambled eggs and bread

- Before shopping for something major, phone around for comparative information.

Media

- Before housecleaning, look over your letters-to-be-answered. During housecleaning, answer the letters in your mind and jot down on a list the main ideas.
- Carry stamped postcards in your purse—for waiting at the doctor's office, etc.
- Store some of your magazines and newsletters by the toilet, others by the telephone, others anywhere else where you pause in the house.
- Don't read anything until you decide what reading is most important for you long-term: then reach for that when you're tempted to read something lighter. (Keep the lighter things in the rack by your toilet or your telephone for quick five-minute glances.)
- Ditto for TV watching. Decide first what you ought to watch this week.
- Skim a book before you read it. Just read the first sentence of every paragraph all the way through the book. By that time you'll know which section of the book you need most—or whether you need it at all. Ultimately, it saves time and you remember the material better.
- Keep a Bible open to the same chapter in every room of the house. As you flit from one room to another, read the next verse. (Seriously, this is how one missionary mother says she does all her Bible study!)
- Review memorized Scripture in the car with your kids. Make it a regular routine, like brushing teeth. (It really works.)

General Organization

- Enjoy small: Plant one pot of flowers, rotating with the seasons, instead of a whole garden of flowers.
- If you're feeling draggy, take a five-minute rest with your feet up every hour.
- An hour before dinner, make yourself a big mug of tea with milk and sugar; or try yogurt, or eggnog.

This will give you needed extra energy as well as dampen your appetite.

- Give yourself deadlines for all activities. Even if you miss them, the deadline will spur you to more vigor.
- Hire somebody to help you a few hours a week. Don't look at it as wasting money; look at it as helping out the unemployment picture.
- Keep your list-book by your bed at night in case you get any crucial ideas while you're half asleep.
- Kinds of lists you might keep:

>main floor housework
>upstairs housework
>basement housework
>yard work
>letters
>calls
>projects
>prayer requests
>shopping (organized by type)
>gifts
>to do while all kids are napping
>to do while baby is napping, others awake
>special activities for myself
>   (various categories)

schedule. Then at the end of the week I review what happened in relation to these guidelines. This pushes me to take initiative in areas that I would let slide otherwise. For example, I may call a rarely-seen friend and say, "Can we get together? While setting up my priorities for this week I discovered that you are a luxury I'd like to treat myself to."

Beyond this, if you're committing yourself to a lonely, unusual, or difficult activity, a list of specific motivators may help. Writing is one of my priorities. But when I get writer's block I lose my nerve and want to withdraw into my shell. To attack that block, I remind myself of these motivations:

Personal call: A conviction that God wants me to write.

Past use: People have been helped by my writing.

Present use: When I get discouraged about what I'm working on now, I remember that when I speak on this material people are helped. So it must be written.

World need: Beyond individuals, the hurting world needs my vision and my creativity expressed.

Models: Isaiah, Catherine Booth, and certain contemporary friends have spent long, lonely, late nights struggling to find the right words. I'm not alone. In their company—even across thousands of miles, or across centuries—I can do it too.

Daily goals: "How do you manage to keep going when writer's block hits?" Philip Yancey, contemporary Christian writer, was asked that question recently. He answered, "Rigid discipline. And then after a few days I get so exasperated with myself that the block disappears."

Public accountability: I seek assignments. I also commit myself to show a friend a certain amount of work by a certain date.

Try undergirding yourself with a similar list of motivators as you "expect great things from God, and attempt great things for God."

In the area of housework and general life maintenance, we can always find simpler strategies. On pages 58-60 I've included a chart with some helpful tips for streamlining household tasks. Most of these are small no's that can free us up to say yes to bigger challenges.

"No" Is a Knife

Over my desk hangs a motto: "Writing is planned neglect." Recently I read a related statement: "Only the unemployed can run for President." Only those who turn down standard activities will have the time and energy to pour into priority affairs.

In the final analysis, all significant living is planned neglect. Ultimately, only a few things can be priorities. It is good to put on leotards, to stretch and to kick, for example. Bodily exercise profits a little. But it is not only good, it is essential to follow Isaiah's advice regarding inner as well as outer discipline. "Awake, awake! Put on your strength . . . put on your beautiful garments . . ." (Isaiah 52:1 NKJV).

A woman's normal life is flooded with distractions, as Anne Morrow Lindbergh observed. What a very hard struggle it is to be a responsible person, as Catherine Booth noted.

Although, or rather, because both of these women knew well how to say no, both are remembered for their positive gifts to the world.

No is a knife word. We cringe from its sharpness. We fear cutting away alternate possibilities. We fear letting go. Yet we need it. Let's remember, there is no fear in God's love (1 John 4:18). And God's love is the context within which we make choices. Why do we say no? In order to say yes to what really matters.

1. Anne Morrow Lindbergh, *Gift from the Sea* (New York: Pantheon, 1955).
2. Catherine Bramwell-Booth, *Catherine Booth* (London: Hodder and Stoughton, 1970), pp. 160-168, 341.
3. Beverly Sills, Commencement Address at Barnard College, quoted in *Time*, June 15, 1981, p. 54.
4. Ruth Klassen, *How Green Is My Mountain* (Downers Grove, Ill.: InterVarsity Press, 1979), pp. 37-39.
5. Ellen Seton, "Women's Fib: You Can Have It All" *Redbook*, February 1984, p. 160.
6. Natalie Shainess, *Sweet Suffering* (New York: Bobbs-Merrill, 1984).

WOMEN AS AMBASSADORS

The Love Mandate

Hagar.

Do you remember her story?

A single mother about 2000 B.C. Illiterate. Originally a slave, chattel, at the bottom of the heap. Sarah's property.

But Sarah was infertile. So after heartbreaking years struggling to get pregnant, determined somehow to have children in the household, Sarah did the next best thing: She pushed Hagar at Abraham, her husband.

Then the trouble began.

As soon as Hagar got pregnant, Sarah regretted her move and started shoving Hagar around. Hagar couldn't take it. She ran off into the desert.

Then, we read, God stopped her—with his presence and with his promises.

How did Hagar respond? She said, "God, you see me" (Genesis 16:13).

Hagar became aware that in spite of all that desert wilderness, in spite of her world's social structure in which she was zilch, God saw her. God knew her as an individual. She was not alone in the universe. She was a creature of God.

This changed Hagar. She acted on God's promises. She switched direction, turned around, went back, and was obedient to Sarah.

Until fourteen years later, when she got kicked out again—this time for good. She hiked with her boy, but there was no passing truck on which they could hitch a ride. They drank all the water. Hagar thrust her boy under one of the desert shrubs. Then she went and sat a good distance away because, she said, "I can't watch my boy die."

Then she howled.

"What's the matter, Hagar?" Once again God startled her. "Don't be afraid. I've heard the voice of your boy, right where he is. Get up. Lift him up. I've got a great future for him."

"Then God opened her eyes, and she saw a well of water" (Genesis 21:19).

A WELL IN ASHRAF'S WILDERNESS

Two years ago, God let me see him provide a well in the wilderness for one of Hagar's daughters—and even let me be a small part of the process.[1] I needed a part-time babysitter for six weeks. A job placement service called. "We have an Iranian woman here who would like to apply to be your babysitter. Her English is so-so. Her highschool-age son is translating for her."

"Well, the job is just part-time. And only for six weeks," I apologized. "I doubt that would be enough for her."

"Hang on just a minute . . ." Mumble, mumble . . . "Hello. She says she'd like to come anyway."

Ashraf came out all by herself, negotiating the city bus network. Interviewing her, I discovered a warm, vibrant, intelligent, and experienced mother in her late thirties. She became our babysitter. During those six weeks I began to learn about her situation. She had come to the U.S. with two young children, probably to keep her son out of the army. Her husband, who had a good job in Iran, planned to send her money regularly. But once she got here he discovered he couldn't get funds out of the country. So here she was, without connections, without funds, without much English, and without street skills. A woman from a sheltered and comfortable background—the sole support of two children.

The six weeks drew to a close. My main babysitter was coming back. Reluctantly, I began to think about Ashraf's future. Had it been any time but December I could probably have let her go and buried any qualms under my preoccupation with the next day's crises. But it was December. I was decorating my house and playing Christmas music. Ashraf's language tutor had gotten her a Farsi language Bible. She was reading it, and telling me how beautiful the story of Jesus was. How could I push her out to starve?

I'm going to have to get her a long-term job, I thought, appalled. (As an absent-minded professor I don't know if I could get *myself* a job.)

Nevertheless, I discussed possibilities with Ashraf. Then, as enthusiastically as Jonah preaching to the Ninevites, I procured neighborhood newspapers from the districts of town near Ashraf's apartment, found "Babysitter Wanted" ads, and started phoning.

"Hello? I'm calling in response to your ad for a babysitter. I'm speaking on behalf of an excellent caregiver, who, however, can't come to the phone."

Believe me, I felt like a fool. But the third person I called hired Ashraf for a full-time job taking care of a four month old. For the past two years that job has kept Ashraf and her children from starving. Meanwhile, the infant is lavished with care: all Ashraf's desire to communicate, which finds so little outlet because of her poor English, is channeled into acts of love for this baby. Her employers have come to value her worth. Even when they go on vacation they take her and her small daughter with them.

That job procurement happened in December. Ashraf continued reading the New Testament. By February, she discovered that she was becoming a follower of Jesus. He was becoming her Lord.

So she telephoned her husband in Iran and asked his permission to be baptized as a Christian.

He gave permission.

In March, a beautiful baptismal service took place with members of various ministries to internationals participating because Ashraf had been blessed by several. She was radiant. Some of the songs and Scripture readings were in Farsi language and some in English. Christian Iranians were present, and non-Christian Iranians. When it came time for her testimony, Ashraf gave it in Farsi language and a Christian Iranian interpreted.

What did she say? The previous fall, she admitted, she nearly had committed suicide. (Probably because of *my* kids! I thought to myself.)

But what drew her irresistibly was the love of Christians and the beautiful person of the Lord Jesus Christ.

Through Christians, who each did what we were called to do—job procurement, language tutoring, Christian witness—God provided a well in Ashraf's wilderness to meet her needs at every level.

A great story. But what does it have to do with our priorities?

REMEBERING HOW GOD HELPED ME

It is my dream that every Muslim woman in North America would have the opportunity to have a Christian friend. That we would make such friendships a top item on our agendas.

As human beings we are commissioned to subdue the earth and have dominion over it. But we've also received a second commission: to be ambassadors for Christ (2 Corinthians 5:17-21 NEB):

> When anyone is united to Christ, there is a new world; the old order has gone, and a new order has already begun. From first to last this has been the work of God. He has reconciled us men to himself through Christ, and he has enlisted us in this service of reconciliation. What I mean is, that God was in Christ reconciling the world to himself, no longer holding men's misdeeds against them, and that he has entrusted us with the message of reconciliation. We come therefore as Christ's ambassadors. It is as if God were appealing to you through us: in Christ's name, we implore you, be reconciled to God! Christ was innocent of sin, and yet for our sake God made him one with the sinfulness of men, so that in him we might be made one with the goodness of God himself.

To help women with crisis pregnancies, to show forth God's reign in the various areas of life around us—these are priority involvements. But they go only part way. Like Hagar, like Ashraf, there have been times when we've been lost in a wilderness. God has dug us wells. The strength and comfort we have today are because of that. True Christian empathy means remembering God's personal grace to us in need, and then reaching out to share it with someone else. It means talking not just about prayer, not just about God, but about the Lord Jesus Christ. He has brought us into personal touch with God. He has introduced us to God's people. He has electrified us with his Holy Spirit.

"Do not withhold good from those to whom it is due, when it is in your power to do it" warned the writer of Proverbs (3:27 NAS).

Is it within our power to talk about the Lord Jesus?

Suppose you made evangelism a priority. You could share Christ with your next door neighbor. You could support overseas missionaries. But suppose you also tried to befriend someone from a culture where there are very few Christians. Someone like Ashraf.

There are many Chinese Christians today. Many Nigerian Christians. Many Filipino Christians. Many Mexican Christians. These people have strong national churches, Bible seminaries, Christian publishers, indigenous theologians. In contrast with these stand "unreached peoples," where very few have heard about the Lord Jesus.

Yet, in the providence of God, all kinds of people are immigrants or visitors to North America today. That means members of "unreached peoples" too. Like many Muslim women.

But suppose you decided God wanted you to focus your energies on a woman like this. How would you go about it?

HOW TO BEFRIEND AN INTERNATIONAL

First you must find an international friend. A university or college will have an international students' advisor who will welcome Americans who want to befriend internationals. Often there is a formal program to match such friendly Americans with newcomers.

At Washington State University, for example, there is an international women's club which whirls with activities: cooking classes, English tutoring, social events. Christian women have been active in the leadership, periodically serving as officers. A great many international student wives have been rescued from loneliness and culture shock, and not a few have taken a sustained look at what it means to be a Christian.

Your city hall, or your newspaper, may have information

on ethnic community organizations, centers, and events. A good place to start is by asking your librarian.

Christian organizations like International Students Incorporated or Association of Christian Ministries to Internationals[2] may well have staff in your area who are in contact with far more lonely internationals than they can handle. Your denomination may have a local ministry to internationals. There are also university ministries like Inter-Varsity, Campus Crusade for Christ, and Navigators which may be reaching out to internationals and may be in need of help locally. As well, many ethnic groups have specialized organizations focusing on them—like the Iranian Followers of Jesus or the Jews for Jesus. There may be an appropriate church or fellowship in your area—Spanish-speaking or Cambodian or Ethiopian.

Once you have attended some ethnic events and have begun to know a few people, maybe the Lord will guide you to friendship with a woman like Ashraf.

After you have found an international friend, *plan how you will spend your time together.* If she speaks little English, these activities may smooth your first visits:

- Take a three-by-five-inch index card listing your name, address, and phone number.
- Take a small gift, like fruit or flowers.
- Take a small family photo album, including pictures of your parents, grandparents, brothers and sisters, children, nieces and nephews, and places where you have lived. This may inspire her to share photos of her family.
- If you enjoy a craft which is easily transportable, like embroidery or carving, take this along. It will help to make the atmosphere more informal, give you something specific to talk about, and may encourage her to bring out some project that she is working on.
- Take paper and pens so that you and she can draw pictures of what you lack words for.
- A map of the world may be familiar to her. If so, she can trace for you the routes of her journeys,

point out where her various friends and relatives are currently living, etc. You too may trace the migrations of your ancestors and your own moves from place to place.

- A Sears catalog often draws shy housewives into conversation.
- Take nonverbal games, which include puzzles, dominoes, chess, etc.
- How-to books, written on practical subjects like baby care or car mechanics, and illustrated with lots of diagrams and photos, may spark interest.
- A cassette of music, a musical instrument, slides or home movies are other possibilities.
- Handicraft material for the children of the family—even simple Play Doh—may provide entertainment for all.
- You may take turns learning bits of each other's language—the numbers from one to ten, names for common objects, etc. Putting yourself in a learning situation similar to hers may expand your empathy as well as her entertainment.

Depending on your friend's interests and responsibilities, here are some activities you might do together:[3]

shopping
feeding ducks
scenic drives, stopping for walks
    at points of interest
garage sales
watching the sunset
cooking, baking, canning
pizza
berry picking
community fairs
watching TV or videos
museums
concerts
table games
parks
sports—badminton, bowling, swimming,
    tennis, fishing, Ping-Pong

But life is more than social events. With any daughter of Hagar, with any friend at all, this is what I want to share: Relationship with God through Christ. The whole counsel of God. The Bible, alive.

Do I know, then . . .

How to get acquainted with a stranger?
How to throw a fun party?
How to turn a conversation to talk about Christ's power to change my life?
How to help someone become a follower of Jesus?
How to respond to common objections to Christianity?
How to study a Bible passage?
How to lead a Bible study?
How to encourage and disciple a new Christian?

These are Christian outreach disciplines. As I get ready to befriend a foreigner, I should set specific goals for my own growth in the skills above—especially those where I'm weak.

Here are some areas where my friend may need teaching:

Old Testament
New Testament
False cults and religions
Christian disciplines: Bible study, prayer, fellowship, witness
Christian ethics, with special attention to cross-cultural dilemmas in adapting to America
Church history, especially vital Christianity in her own country

Certainly I don't know everything about the Christian view of the family or politics or Buddhism. In fact, in discussion with my friend over the open Bible, I may learn a lot.

How do I, myself, learn to grasp Bible truths? We'll explore that in the next chapter. In this chapter, we'll play with another question: What should I know about my friend's culture? I want to discuss this in some detail. At first this may seem like a tangent in a book focusing on American woman. But I believe there are few greater opportunities and priorities facing American Christian women today than reaching out to our international neighbors.

I'm going to suggest five aspects of culture to explore. These are: family, social structure, communication styles, economy, and religion and values.

FAMILY: I KNOW I'LL BE MARRIED BUT I DON'T KNOW TO WHOM

Once, when I was visiting the Philippines, I stayed in a young woman's apartment. She was household head for several younger brothers, sisters, and nieces living temporarily in the city. In the evening I had to go across town to a meeting.

"Donny," said my hostess to her twenty-five-year-old brother, "please accompany Miriam across town."

Donny had been lounging in front of the TV in complete comfort.

I was mortified. How could she so impose on him?

But without hesitation he levered himself out of the chair and got ready to take the bus with me. (It wasn't safe for an unaccompanied woman like me to be out alone at night.)

Who of us would have dared to ask our adult brother to give up his evening for a stranger like that? Yet I'm convinced that Donny didn't mind seriously. It didn't occur to him to mind. In his country, older relatives give up a lot for younger ones. My hostess, an editor, desperately needed a peaceful and quiet apartment. Instead she had to supervise the capricious moral dilemmas of a half dozen young adult relatives. By the same token, younger kin like Donny automatically jump to help when an older one asks for it.

This family arrangement is different from ours. We maximize husband-wife relationships, and then parent-child relationships. We minimize everything else. But even in the favored relationships we emphasize independence. I have Filipino friends whose children sleep in the parents' bed until they are three. Even after that, Filipinos never have to sleep in a room alone.

I also have a friend from India. She is a college teacher, from a Christian family. However, her marriage was arranged by her parents. And she and her well-educated Christian husband like that approach to marriage.

Once I asked her, "When you quit teaching a year before your wedding, did you know you were going to be married?"

"Yes," she answered, "but I didn't know to whom."

What a different world—to be sure that you will be married but to have no idea who your husband will be. To trust your family to take care of that. And to assume that you will adjust to him, whoever he is.

As you get to know a woman from another country, be aware that these kinds of experiences may make her family life different from yours.

Social Structure: Pay My Fare, Too

Ariel, another Filipino friend, found work in a country far from home. She ended up living with some Americans, Christian women like herself.

"Unfortunately," she confided to me, "they're not very Christian."

"Why?" I asked, rather surprised, because I knew that these Americans were quite dedicated.

"Why, whenever we get on a bus, they pay only their own fares."

A revelation swept over me. Of course! When a group of Filipino friends board a bus, the first one always pays the fares for all, even if it bankrupts him. They live from feast to famine—each one alternately providing the feast.

Like many other peoples, Filipinos have a stronger sense of groupness and rootedness than we do. We Americans are mobile, both upwardly and geographically. We leave our birth families behind. Then we join voluntary organizations to make up for the lack of the extended family.

A few years ago, when the economy was more depressed, *Time* magazine featured a story about young single adults in the U.S. moving back into their parents' homes. Letters of protest shot in to *Time*: "This will never work. The young adults will be stifled, and even the parents will lose their freedom and individuality."

I had to chuckle because I had just been interviewing a Vietnamese pastor, an immigrant to the U.S., who had told me that unmarried adults ought to live in their parents' homes. In his culture they usually turn over their salary to their mother, receiving only an allowance. Parents "have experience," they "see further than their children," I was told. Adult children need their parents' wisdom, and in return parents deserve to have their children close so they can participate vicariously in their youth and vitality.

Most peoples have a stronger sense of groupness, less emphasis on self-reliance than we do.

An American friend whose daughters are four and eight told me that her girls do a good deal of the housecleaning. With three young sons, I found this hard to imagine.

"Oh, I pay them pretty well," she said. Then she reflected, "Last year they did things around the house just to please me. But now they're beginning to grasp the idea of money. They plan what they want to buy. They count their earnings. They strategize. I'm really pleased with their development," she smiled.

I gulped. How many societies there are where people work all their lives primarily to please a boss or an elder—not just to make a private income. Yet we consider it "development" when our young children show this kind of self-focused thinking.

As you get to know a woman from another culture, resist the tendency to view her as an isolated individual. Instead, consider this: What are the important groups in which she is rooted? Ask regularly about her family, including those overseas. Get to know some of the fellow-countrymen she associates with here. It takes a lot more courage to befriend ten Libyans than one Libyan. But given most peoples' group orientation, it is important. As well as inviting her to things, allow her to invite you. Go so far as to be willing to be her guest at parties where little English is spoken, where you are vulnerable and dependent, where she controls the turf. That kind of exchange fosters true reciprocity and friendship.

Muslim theology makes a strong emphasis on the *Ummah*, a concept something like the "people of God" or the "kingdom of God." A Muslim woman is raised within the security of this community. To such a person we dare not demonstrate merely an individualistic Christianity. We must show our interdependence with other Christians, our awareness that we as individuals do not have all the gifts but are merely small facets of God's kaleidoscope. Because our Muslim friend comes from a universal tradition that demands international brotherhood and sisterhood, we must not be local or provincial in our view of Christianity either. We must live and walk in such a way that we transmit a sense of the family of God around the world.

And if our Muslim friend comes to faith in Christ, we must care for her need for corporate fellowship. But not necessarily "Christian" fellowship. Some fellowships of former Muslims don't call themselves "Christians." That word has centuries of bad connotations, from the Crusades onward. Rather, they call themselves "Followers of Jesus."

COMMUNICATION: MESS UP YOUR FLOWERS

A girl from India traveled to the U.S. as an exchange student. Her host family met her at the airport, whisked her home, and welcomed her to their house.

"How was your trip?" they asked. They showed her her room and the rest of the house. They discussed her future school and other activities. They inquired about her family.

In the course of their conversation the mother said, "As

it happens, we all ate some time ago, but I have some supper set aside for you that I'll bring out in a minute if you'd like it."

"Oh no, please don't bother," the Indian girl said.

"Really? Are you sure?" the mother wondered.

"No, please, that's quite unnecessary," the girl assured her.

"Well . . ." the mother shrugged, and the conversation moved on. Years later, that girl told her American college roommate that she had cried herself to sleep that night because she was so hungry. Apparently, due to nervousness and tight travel schedules, she hadn't eaten for a day.

Why this missed communication? In the girl's background, a person didn't accept an invitation unless it was pressed several times. Quite a number of peoples follow this custom. With them a message has to be given incrementally, in repeated installments.

Incremental communication is something we may need to learn as we befriend someone from another culture.

Indirect communication is another lesson. In Japan, says a Japanese author, only an uncouth person needs a complete, frank verbal message. If you are a person of any refinement you will find a more indirect, nuanced, euphemistic, metaphorical way to get your point across. For example, suppose a Japanese woman has had a hard day with her mother-in-law. How might she communicate this to her husband? Well, she might arrange the flowers in front of the door in a haphazard way. When her husband comes home, he sees that the flowers are disarranged. He realizes that his wife is at her wits' end, and concludes that this is probably because of his mother, who lives in. So he's more tolerant with his wife that evening.[4]

Many cultures prefer indirect communication. Mexicans, for example, have asked us Americans, "Why are you so frank, when you could be courteous?" Then we realize we had not thought of indirectness as a virtue.

The communication styles that people are comfortable with should shape our Christian communication.

ECONOMICS: COWS AND EARRINGS

Now let's consider economies: the physical sphere of life. Bargains. Coupons. Sales. Hand-me-downs. Shopping. Christmas cookie exchanges. Not to mention investment portfolios, stocks, IRA's, CD's.

Should you can fruits and vegetables? Or spend the time shopping at discount stores? Or spend the time earning in a part-time job so you don't have to be so pinchpenny?

Man can't live by bread alone, but man does need bread. Our families' stomachs are time-bombs that have to be reset regularly, or they will explode.

How do women in various cultures handle this part of life? In different ways. Make no mistake though. Production, procurement, and exchange play a big part in their worries. To empathize with your friend, you must grope toward an understanding of what economic strategies she feels comfortable with.

You might be surprised to learn that even traditional women have exercised economic power in many societies. Take Umm Ahmad, a peasant Egyptian, a Muslim. Recently her young married daughter, Habibah, came to her with a question.

"Mother, Muhammad and Farouq want me to sell my gold earrings."

"Why?" Umm Ahmad asked.

"So they can buy a cow," Habibah answered, "as a shared investment between the two of them."

"Hmph."

"What do you think?" Habibah persisted. "After all, they're my brother and my husband."

"I wouldn't advise it, my girl," Umm Ahmad shook her head firmly. "No, I definitely would not advise it at all. You'd be a fool to let that capital slip through your fingers."

Habibah took heed. Muhammad and Farouq got no cow

out of that deal. A few months later, however, Umm Ahmad took Habibah aside. "I have a suggestion. Why don't you sell your gold earrings and buy a calf in partnership with Muhammad and Farouq?"

"Well . . ."

"Just make sure—" Umm Ahmad added, "Just make sure you get a signed receipt from Farouq for the amount of money you lend him. And then buy yourself a small pair of earrings with whatever you have left."

Although a Muslim, and therefore viewed by many of us Westerners as subordinated and limited in her options as a woman, Umm Ahmad showed considerable managerial prowess throughout her life. She rotated the house and field work between her daughters and daughters-in-law. All her sons gave her their income. She bought their food, their clothes, and the family seed and fertilizer. For a time she ran a small store. Whenever one of her sons wanted to get married, Umm Ahmad would sell the family buffalo. After the wedding, with the gifts guests had contributed, Umm Ahmad would buy a buffalo calf.[5]

Such skills are not unusual. Souvanni, a Cambodian immigrant to the U.S., recently married off the second of her several children. This required three elaborate ceremonies, each with new clothes for all the bridal party: the traditional Cambodian wedding ceremony, the ten-course Chinese dinner for 350 people, and the church wedding.

For the restaurant alone, Souvanni paid $6,000.

But that same night she collected $7,000. Cambodian custom calls for the bridal party to make their way from table to table, bowing and greeting. Each table of people stands to their feet, bowing and pronouncing blessing on the new couple. Meanwhile, the guests slip to the mother of the groom a white envelope which has been beside their forks. These envelopes contain money gifts. So Souvanni, like women in many cultures, manages to gather respectable funds to put on a wedding.

Economics involves consumption. When I was living in the Philippines, a close friend watching me cook one day blurted out, "You use salt? How extravagant!"

Extravagant? I wondered. What next?

"What in the world do you use then?" I retorted.

"Fish sauce, of course," he said.

I, too, had fish sauce, but I had used it to salt what I thought were appropriate dishes, not scrambled eggs or oatmeal.

That day I learned that physical things as simple as salt are not viewed the same everywhere.

VALUES AND RELIGION: DIRTY WINDOWS

Culture's Consequences: International Differences in Work-Related Values by Geert Hofstede is a study of the values of IBM employees in fifty countries. Japanese employees, he finds, work best with clear rules and hierarchy. German employees are comfortable with rules but expect bosses and workers to negotiate on an equal basis. Indonesians, on the other hand, are proud of bosses who behave with the dignity, decisive authority, and expense accounts of top brass, as they are pleased with employees who can adapt flexibly to variables that change frequently. Americans value informality, frankness, egalitarianism, and adjustable negotiations.[6]

Joan and Ted Abbott learned about German values when they spent a couple of years in Germany setting up a Christian ministry. One of their trips took them away from their apartment for five weeks. It was good to get back and begin to unpack. They hadn't been home twenty minutes, though, when there was a knock on the door.

"Good day, Frau Abbott," said the woman from across the hall. "Welcome back."

"Oh Frau Snelling, please do come in."

After a few minutes of small talk, Frau Snelling came to

the real point of her visit. "Frau Abbott, I must speak to you about your windows."

Joan knew her neighbors washed their windows twice a week. When home, she or Ted tried to do theirs once a week and felt like heroes. But now—

"Yes, I'm so sorry, I know they're dirty. But you know, I've been away for five weeks, and only just got in," Joan began.

"But you could have hired somebody," Frau Snelling insisted. Then she added her final blow: "And you a Christian!"

In the German culture, order and routine are valued. To shine as lights in their community, the Abbotts couldn't laugh this off.

As I get to know a woman from another culture, I should expect that her values will channel her behavior differently from mine.

In the area of religion, for example, Muslims value the concept of God. While many people around the world are becoming secular humanists, Muslims stand firm. "There is no God but God." That is part of the Muslim creed, recited five times daily. Emerging against a background of rampant idolatry, the prophet Muhammad's idea of one God sparkles like a diamond. It is a lofty concept. Muslims do not worship God with flippant and thoughtless "Hallelu, hallelu, hallelu, hallelujah, praise ye the Lord" choruses. Instead, they wash their hands and feet before entering a mosque, to symbolize that we must be clean before a holy God. A Muslim woman may be involved on a day-to-day basis with propitiating spirits, but if she knows much of her religion she also will hold a high concept of God.

But is the God of Islam the God of the Bible? Certainly their God is incomplete. He is too distant. Although he reveals himself in Scripture and through prophets, he would never lower himself to become man. That would be blasphemy to a Muslim.

Nevertheless, converts from Islam don't think they are coming to a new God when they meet the Father of our Lord Jesus

Christ. Rather, they feel completed. They feel that the one whom they worshiped in ignorance, inaccurately and incompletely—this one has now become their personal father.

As with Muslims' appreciation of community and high view of God, there are many values and doctrines in any heritage, including the Muslim, which can become bridges for communicating Christ. Abraham's sacrifice of his son. Christ as servant. Christ as prophetic teacher. All of these are found in the Muslim holy book, the Quran, and all can be bridges.

HAGAR HASN'T SEEN THE END YET

Family, social structure, communication styles, economy, and religion and values are five aspects of culture to explore as we get to know a woman from another culture, motivated because we want to share Christ with her. (In the Appendix are Cultural Research Questions to guide more specific observations in each of these areas.)

Befriending a woman from another culture adds interest and challenge to our lives. It broadens us. Such friendships multiplied many times over go a long way to contribute to a more peaceful community and even to a more peaceful world as peoples build bridges and develop some degree of trust.

Interesting, challenging, peacemaking involvements are not our first focus in this chapter, however. We women are called to be ambassadors of the Lord Jesus. How easy it is to snuggle down into comfortable routines. How hard to risk new relationships, especially across cultural gaps. When things are going okay we repress memories of those wilderness days when God dug wells for us. Are we embarrassed to admit that we were ever so vulnerable?

To the lukewarm church in Laodicea, God said, "You say, 'I am rich; I have acquired wealth and do not need a thing.' But you do not realize that you are wretched, pitiful, poor, blind and naked. I counsel you to buy from me gold refined in the fire, so you can become rich. . . ." (Revelation 3:17-18).

Because God has commissioned us not to be robots but to love our neighbors; because there are few more needy neighbors than those who come from cultures where they can't hear about Christ; because some of these people now live conveniently in our vicinity; because day by day God empowers us with grace and with confidence, we dare to befriend a strange foreigner.

Hagar hasn't seen the end yet. After she and her son drank from God's well in the wilderness four thousand years ago, they went on and prospered. The boy grew and became a strong warrior. Hagar got him a wife from Egypt, and he had sons and daughters. And some of these sons are mentioned in Isaiah 60 where we read about the peoples of the earth coming to the throne to give God homage at the end of time. We read about Nabaioth, Hagar's first grandson, and Kedar, another grandson, coming in that great procession and bringing sacrifices that will be acceptable upon God's altar.

Right now we can reach out to Hagar's daughters in our own city and show them how to come acceptably to God through the Lord Jesus Christ.

Hagar hasn't seen the end yet.

1. Muslims see themselves as descended from Abraham and Sarah. Although Iranians are not Arabs, they trace their symbolic roots to Abraham, as we Christians do.

2. Association of Church Mission Committees
P.O. Box ACMC
Wheaton, IL 60189
312-260-1660

International Students, Inc.
Star Ranch
P.O. Box C
Colorado Springs, CO 80901
303-576-2700

Navigators
P.O. Box 6000
Colorado Springs, CO 80934
303-598-1212

Inter-Varsity Christian Fellowship
233 Langdon
Madison, Wisconsin 53703
608-274-9001

Campus Crusade, International
Arrowhead Springs
San Bernardino, CA 92414
714-886-5224

3. Joyce Davenport lives in Seattle, Washington. This partial list devised by her is used with permission.

4. Takie Sugiyama Lebra, *Japanese Patterns of Behavior* (Honolulu: University Press of Hawaii, 1976), p. 47.

5. Lucie Wood Saunders, "Umm Ahmad, A Village Mother of Egypt," in *Middle Eastern Muslim Women Speak*, eds. Elizabeth Fernea and Basima Qattan Bezirgan (Austin, Tex.: University of Texas Press, 1977), pp. 221-30.

6. Geert Hofstede, *Culture's Consequences: International Differences in Work-Related Values* (Beverly Hills, Calif.: Sage Publications, 1980).

6

SAYING YES

Fire in Our Bones

January. My head splinters, especially at Arsenic Hour, 5:00 P.M. Thank God for Mister Rogers. The boys clang with post-Christmas jitters: toys, candy, excitement. They demand, they clamor all at once and incessantly, they tug on my shirt and hang at my heels. Can they occupy themselves? Can they be quiet? No way. Cooped up, they go stir crazy.

Three A.M.: Shall I get up and see if baby is breathing? One shrill week in isolation with Joel, and now baby has succumbed to the flu. Can I stand it? Ha! I haven't seen anything yet. Count on three more weeks: Daniel, Michael, and last of all myself.

Nature, like our bank account, is deflated, battened down. The fall leaves underfoot are not pretty. They have long since turned to sludge. This is the month when old people die and babies catch dangerous bugs.

I dread Januarys. So I try to develop some special coping mechanisms for that month. Maybe *your* Januarys come in June. We all have those low points when all the waves and billows of the world seem to be breaking over us.

In a less extreme way, not only our low points but also many of the stretches of our lives yawn like the twilight zone of January. We live inhibited. We live "lives of quiet desperation." We live hemmed in by our circumstances, and our sins.

Maybe you weren't loved enough as a child. Or maybe you've messed up your marriage. Your job. Your spiritual life. Your body. Maybe you feel a failure in your loneliness. Maybe your children are not what you'd hoped they'd be.

TV and magazines tell us we're creative, beautiful, and ought to assert ourselves. God agrees. We're made in his image, lovely. But that's not the whole picture. A Christian view of human nature is that we're not only in God's image, we're also sinners. We're not only unique and creative, we're also selfish, lazy, and intimidated. By our selfishness, we mess up the world.

How can God love you? And use you? When I look in the mirror I sometimes wonder, How can God use someone thirty pounds overweight?

But what is my value based on? My looks? My background? My accomplishments? No, I'm valuable because God has given me personality, modeled on his personality. And beyond that, Christ has reached out to me personally and powerfully—and gotten hurt in the process. As one poet has said,

> The other gods were strong, but Thou wast weak,
> They rode, but Thou didst stumble to Thy throne.
> To our wounds but a wounded God can speak,
> And not a God has wounds but Thou alone.[1]

Praise God, we *are* loved. God has made us creative in his image. And beyond that, Jesus has reached out to us powerfully and personally. Believe it, sister. Wake up each morning and immerse yourself in what some have called the most profound Scripture teaching: "Jesus loves me, this I know, for the Bible tells me so." Remind yourself of it continually. Let's affirm it for each other. How we need this. Then we can stand tall—and reach out. Then we can be active channels of God's grace rather than ticking out our days in quiet resignation. Then we will not be afraid to be assertive.

I am convinced that the great need of women today is to know the love of God and experience it deeply. Only God's love is hot enough to melt our inhibitions.

It's by the grace of God, by the forgiving love of God, by the restoring activity of God, that we live.

How can we know God with this intensity year round? Two classic disciplines help: Bible study and prayer.

BIBLE STUDY: MY PEOPLE, MY ROOTS

The Bible is not primarily doctrines. It is primarily the stories of people who have known God. Role models. For better or for worse.

Who am I? we ask from time to time. I am a woman. An American. Maybe I identify myself by my profession. My favorite sports and hobbies. My age bracket. Marital status. Family background. In a sense I am also asking, Who are my people? The groups we identify with constitute our reference groups. Each of us may have several such groups. We may differ. I may be a bowler. You may be a singer. But as Christians we should have at least one reference group in common—the people throughout history who have known God.

These folks experienced the same troubles and temptations that we do. Like David in the Psalms, we experience doubt. Like Jeremiah, we experience despair. Like Solomon, we may have roving eyes sexually. Like Abraham, we may experience a derailed career. Like Esther, we may be confronted with overwhelming odds. Like Hagar, we may be rejected.

These biblical characters sinned. Yet they found God real and relevant not just in their holy moods but also in their troubles and sins. This comforts me. When I find myself surrounded by troubles outside and sins inside, I remember my spiritual forefathers and mothers and realize again that nothing can separate me from the love of God. From such a variety of personalities in the Bible—farmers, soldiers, scholars, religious workers, mothers, childless women, prostitutes, eunuchs—there are many lessons for us. Some of these people may seem strange with their battles, many wives, child sacrifices, and idols. But they are measured by how well they served their generation according to the will of God. We, too, are measured by that. By observing how they served their neighbors—what they did right and what they didn't, when they listened to God and when they ran away—we can learn better how to serve our time.

How do I grasp Bible truths? Do I pray, flip open the Bible on my knees with my eyes closed, poke in my finger, open my eyes, read the verse where my finger lies and take that as God's authoritative word on the problem I'm wrestling with?

Some people do that. One man in a dilemma about what he should do with his life prayed earnestly, then parted the Bible to see what verse God would give him.

"Judas went and hanged himself," he read.

Is that my model? he thought, mortified. I must have messed up the technique.

So he tried again.

"Go thou and do likewise," said the new verse.

Chagrinned, and sincerely seeking guidance, he flipped the pages once more.

"What thou doest, do quickly," said the Scripture.

Understanding God's teaching is not magic. God has given us minds, and told us to use these to grasp his Word. It's true that we are ignoramuses compared with God. Yet he wants us to be wise. "Come now, let us reason together," God says through Isaiah (1:18). "My people are destroyed from lack of knowledge," he says through Hosea (4:6). "Since the first day that you set your mind to gain understanding . . . your words were heard," Daniel is told (10:12). Solomon is blessed for wanting wisdom more than anything else (1 Kings 3:11-12). "You know how to interpret the appearance of the sky, but you cannot interpret the signs of the times," Jesus mocks the Pharisees (Matthew 16:3).

In Philippians 1:9-10 Paul commands us to grow in knowledge so as to discern what is excellent. In 1 Corinthians he says, "I will pray with my spirit, but I will *also pray with my mind*" (14:15). As well, he tells us, "In regard to evil be infants, but *in your thinking be adults*" (14:20). In Romans 2, he indicates that we are judged on the basis of our knowledge. Ten times in Romans and Corinthians the question recurs: *"Don't you know? Don't you know?"* Colossians indicates that the goal of Christian leaders is to present every person mature in Christ, *with all wisdom* (1:28).[2] We women love God with our hearts. Do we also love him with our minds? Or do we neglect that, feeling he is beyond our rational grasp? Let's remember, our emotions are just as fallen as our minds. And our minds are more easily kept in check.

On pages 92-94 are some commonsense questions to ask of a Bible passage. These are developed by Leticia Magalit in *How to Lead Bible Studies*.[3]

These questions will help us mine the gold from a Bible passage. But if we are to understand the doctrines and teachings of the Bible, we must do even more. Some passages are very difficult. In general, symbolic passages must be interpreted in light of plain teaching passages found elsewhere. Perplexing incidental verses must be viewed in light of the systematic teaching contained in doctrinal books like Romans or Galatians. One Bible passage may turn out to be only a small part of the truth.

Hermeneutics, or procedures of biblical interpretation, can help us make sense of "difficult passages." Listed on pages 94-95 are some "principles of hermeneutics" abstracted from *Protestant Biblical Interpretation* by Bernard Ramm.[4]

Questions for Bible Study

A Narrative Passage

1. *Observe*

- Who are the characters? Describe each as to his title, occupation, role, attitudes, and relationships with others. What is the central action? A conversation? An argument? A miracle? Preaching? Healing?
- Where does the action take place? What is significant about the location?
- When does the action take place? What is significant about the time?
- How is the action carried out? Does it lead up to a climax? What does it reveal about the person doing it?
- Why does the action take place? What is the stated reason? Is there a deeper reason?
- What are the results of the action for the characters?

2. *Interpret*

- Take any fact. Why was this fact given? What does it reveal about the people and the situation of that day?
- What do the characters' words and actions mean?
- What does the whole story teach? What did it mean to the people then?
- What does the story reveal about the character of God, Jesus Christ, the Holy Spirit, and man? How does the story help me understand them better?
- How does the story help me understand God's purpose in history?

3. *Apply*

- What have I learned about God—Father, Son, or Holy Spirit?
- How should I respond to him?
- What sin in my life has been uncovered? What should I do about it?

- What commands have I discovered? How can I obey them in practical ways?
- Are there examples to follow? Or examples to avoid?
- Do I need to change some of my attitudes?
- Are there some promises for me? What conditions must I fulfill to claim them?

A Discourse Passage

1. *Observe*

- Gather general background information. Who wrote this? Why? Who were the original readers? What was their particular situation?
- Look for paragraph divisions. What is the central thought in each paragraph? How is it developed? Note illustrations, examples, quotations, questions, comparisons, or contrasts. If you see any commands, warnings, or promises, list these and try to discover the reasons, conditions, and results associated with them. When an idea is repeated, it may be specially emphasized.
- Connect the paragraphs. Is there a progression of thought?
- Sum up the major truth. Who is saying what to whom in what circumstances?

2. *Interpret*

- What was the author thinking and feeling? What was his attitude toward his readers?
- Which words and phrases are important? What do they mean?
- What truth did the author want to communicate? How did he present it? Why did he put it this way?
- What did this mean to the original readers? How was it supposed to affect their lives?
- What does this teach about God, Christ, or the Holy Spirit?

3. *Apply*

- Imagine that the author is talking directly to you. What do you learn from him? As you ponder these questions, pray that God will open your eyes, mind, and heart.
- What have I found out about God, Christ, or the Holy Spirit?
- How should this affect my relationship with the triune God?
- What sin in my life is pointed out? I must confess it, ask forgiveness, and turn away from it.
- How is the writer an example for me? How can I imitate him?
- Is there any advice or warning especially for me? How can I obey it?
- How does this passage encourage me?
- What have I learned about the kind of relationships I should have with Christians or with non-Christians?
- What makes me want to praise God?

Principles of Hermeneutics

A General Passage

- Take the most natural interpretation.
- Consider the context in which the passage was written: language, culture, historical situation, geographical environment, literary style.
- Interpret progressively in time (i.e. interpret the Old Testament in light of the New Testament, the Gospels in light of the Epistles, etc.).
- Interpret Scripture by Scripture, seeing the Bible as a unity.
- See how the passage relates to God's salvation in Christ.
- Emphasize principles rather than local details.

- When you extend your interpretations beyond the clear teaching of the Bible, do not make these interpretations binding.
- Be willing to accept paradoxes.
- Distinguish between what Scripture records and what it approves.

A Biographical Passage

- Distinguish between what is recorded and what is approved (i.e. David's sins).
- Determine the outstanding spiritual principles illustrated.
- Apply the general principles, not the local details.

Parables

- Determine the central truth. Avoid emphasis on details.
- See if Christ interprets the parable.
- Consider the context: Who is the audience? Why was Christ stimulated to tell the story?
- Compare with parallel passages or with any Old Testament associations.

Prophecy

- Interpret in its original setting first.
- Check if it is interpreted in Scripture, or if there are parallel passages or parallel concepts.
- Don't take symbolic language literally.
- Don't study prophecy just to increase your general knowledge, but rather to increase your knowledge of Christ, so that you can do his will.

LIKE EATING CHOCOLATE CHIP COOKIES

Because one Bible passage alone does not give me a complete picture, I need to search the whole counsel of God in order to build principles for my own Christian world view from the sum of Scripture's teachings. Then when I react to a contemporary issue, I will be guided by the basic truths I have stored up.

That's hopeless! I would never have time for that! we may sigh in despair.

But reading the Bible is not like picking up messes on the floor. Or keypunching the day's program. No, reading the Bible is like meeting a special friend for lunch. Eating chocolate chip cookies. Battling through a game of raquetball. Lazing away a day at the beach. Reading the Bible doesn't drain us. It invigorates. It renews. It recreates us.

All people are like grass, Isaiah wrote in chapter 40. All human beauty wears out. People wither, beauty fades. But the Word of God vibrates through all history, new every morning. That's Isaiah's (chapter 40) and James' (chapter 1) message. As we attach ourselves to that Word—as we immerse ourselves in its message of love from the very Creator and Sustainer of all reality, we too transcend history, transcend our precariously made-up beauty, the loss of friends who move away, children who move out, jobs and projects that fail or grow stale, the limits of our lifespan. We are connected—really—to our dreams that in this life we ourselves will never achieve.

God's Word vibrates through history. It is sharper than any two-edged sword, cutting to the root of our put-ons. It burns our impurities. And having done that, it nurtures life.

> For as the rain cometh down,
> and the snow from heaven,
> and returneth not thither,
> but watereth the earth,
> and maketh it bring forth and bud,
> that it may give seed to the sower,
> and bread to the eater:

So shall my word be
that goeth forth out of my mouth:
It shall not return unto me void,
but it shall accomplish that which I please. . . .
(Isaiah 55:10-11 KJV)

God's Word—the ultimate truths about reality—comes to us beyond books, in the person of Jesus Christ who is also called God's Word (John 1). Through Christ all history, all societies, and all nature are sustained and held together (Colossians 1 and Hebrews 1). As we cultivate a relationship with Christ, we are plunged into essential reality and recharged day by day.

The Lord God hath given me the tongue of the learned, that I should know how to speak a word in season to him that is weary: he wakeneth morning by morning, he wakeneth mine ear to hear as the learned (Isaiah 50:4 KJV).

Our first spiritual discipline for knowing God is Bible study. How else can we escape the limits of our culture's majority view, the limits of our own reason, the limits even of our own Christian fellowship? All of these may be warped by human ignorance and selfishness. We need a guide independent of our culture and our reason. Fortunately, God has given us such a guide in his Word. We must be like the Bereans whom Paul praised because they "examined the Scriptures every day to see if what Paul said was true" (Acts 17:11). And as we take the Bible on our laps, it is an awesome thing to realize that thousands of Russians and Africans and Chinese and Nicaraguans are doing the same thing. We meet together as equals around the Word of God. Together we probe our reference group, our heritage, our roots.

As the book of Hebrews records, when the various Bible characters died, they had not yet received fulfillment of all the promises—because they were waiting for *us*. Because they without us could not be made perfect. They wait—and they are still waiting—for the family to be complete. They call us to interact with God who is dynamic, to participate in the ongoing story.

97

PRAYER: LIGHTING MY CANDLE AT GOD'S FIRE

The year of Grace 1654.
Monday 23 November, feast of St. Clement, pope and martyr,
and of others in the martyrology,
Eve of St. Chrysogonus, martyr, and others,
From about half past ten in the evening to about half an hour
after midnight.

Fire

'God of Abraham, God of Isaac, God of Jacob'
not of the philosophers and learned.
Certitude, Certitude, love, joy, peace
God of Jesus Christ
Deum meum et deum vestrum.
'Thy God shall be my God.'
Forgetfulness of the world and
of everything outside God.
He is not found except by the means taught in the Gospel.
Greatness of the human soul
'Holy Father, the world hath not known Thee, but I have known
Thee.'
Joy, Joy, Joy, tears of joy.[5]

That's how Blaise Pascal described his climactic experience
of God on November 23, 1654. "Fire!" Although he was a
mathematical genius, whose writings are still read by philosophers today, Pascal needed more. He began to research Christianity. His diary traced the journey. When Pascal experienced
God, he found an outlet for rich emotions which mathematics
could not release. God's spirit flamed through him.

"Our God is a consuming fire," wrote the author of
Hebrews. "Take off your shoes: you stand on holy ground,"
Moses was told when he confronted the burning bush of God's
presence. Elijah, in his contest with false prophets, found God
to be the Lord who answers by fire. John Wesley found himself
"strangely warmed" when he came into personal relationship
with God through Christ. Today we sing, "Spirit of God, de-
scend upon my heart . . . [make] my heart an altar, and thy
love the flame." Oh for the fire of God to thaw our Januarys!

For many of us, life is running fairly smoothly. To look at TV ads, or even at our smiley Christian TV preachers and singers, we might get the impression that's how life is. But our crises will come. The deaths of our parents. Unforeseen problems with our children. Cancer. Who knows? The point is, God often uses these breaks in the routine, God often uses our Januarys, as he did with Hagar's desert experiences, to show us himself.

God is scary. He disturbs our routine. He rattles our categories. He is not only the answer to our problems but also the problem to our answers. Christ's resurrection breaks natural law. God's grace for sinners shatters the cause and effect principles by which we live, that what we sow we will reap. Miracles mess up our schedules. How are we supposed to follow the priorities on saying no that we set up in Chapter Four if God keeps disturbing us?

But in our Januarys, when we get into a situation like Hagar's, we find we need a God like that. A God beyond the ordinary. God who is in fact God.

PRAYER: A CHANNELED MIND

It is in prayer that we light our candle at God's fire.

Scripture without the living Holy Spirit is dead letters. We need more than the Bible: we need prayer. This is the second discipline we must cultivate.

But if Scripture needs prayer, prayer also needs Scripture. Prayer that is unfocused is dangerous. Spirit without Scripture can lead us to a cult. Without checking Scripture continually, we can't be sure what spirit we're following.

Joshua is the first person in the Bible who is told to meditate. But he was to meditate on something outside himself: The Word of God, the eternal truths of God, the historic stories of God's encounters with people. Joshua had a channeled mind. He was to meditate on God's Word even in the casual junctures of the day—when he rose up, when he sat down. Centuries later, Isaiah told the people of God to teach their

99

children to meditate on God's word when rising, when sitting, when coming in, when going out. David meditated on God's word in the night watches and found it "sweeter than honey, more precious than gold." Isaiah and Jeremiah ate the Word! Underlying our prayers, then, we are to be immersed in Scripture as in a hot jacuzzi, until it comes out our pores. As we pray, we are to have channeled minds.

"Can you tell me a good book on spirituality?" students frequently ask me. "I've read Henri Nouwen, Thomas Merton, Morton Kelsey, and sections from St. Theresa and John of the Cross . . ."

My answer: "Get a good Bible study book."

In the current craze for spirituality, I fear many are going second class. In their prayer and meditation they are focusing too much on the transcendent, the numinous, the supernatural, on mystical techniques, on the history of meditation. They are not focusing enough on the specific content which is the context for Christian prayer: Scripture, in all its length and breadth.

Spirituality per se is no more to the glory of God than physicality. Spirituality can be prideful, selfish, idolatrous.

Let me be the first to admit, though, that the "spiritual" writers have helped me. As I've grown older, I find myself seeing the forest more than the trees. I used to feel for a particular situation; now I think in abstractions. I used to focus on individuals; now I think of world needs. Drowning in analytical, conceptual, abstract generalizations, now I have to reach for my imagination. I have to exercise it consciously.

Here the writers on spirituality have directed me. In recent years I have learned from them to describe my feelings metaphorically—in terms of senses, colors, textures, in terms of concrete experiences in specific places, with animal or technical or historical images. Morton Kelsey in particular has shown me how to cultivate the imagination by working through a feeling or an idea physically, so as to get below the level of consciousness. Kelsey himself often "thinks" by building sand castles.

As for me, as I have tried to wake up my imagination, certain meditative techniques have helped. In writing, for example, I imagine myself into the skin of a historical writer I admire, like Isaiah or Catherine Booth.

I have benefited from the contemplative writers, the acolytes of spirituality pursued so avidly by some of my most dedicated students. Yet their benefits for prayer are limited. There is a sense in which once you've read one of these books, you've read them all. To keep on brings diminishing returns. When we center down in ourselves, we can only bring up the images that are stored there. Pretty soon we're left wallowing in the shallow pool of our own ignorance. Our prayers start going in circles.

That's why, when someone asks me, "What else should I read on spirituality?" I answer, "Get a good Bible study book."

PRAYER: REFLECTING THE SPARKLE OF SCRIPTURE

But that doesn't mean we pray with imprisoned imaginations. Scripture ripples with metaphors. It was never meant to be understood only analytically and logically. Scripture is stories as much as doctrines. In fact, Scripture is high drama. All the movies of nuclear holocaust—*The Day After*, *Testament*—pale beside the apocalyptic drama of the Old Testament prophets and Revelation. Certainly there are glorious "Holy, Holy, Holy" passages in Scripture. There are also absurdities. Consider Ezekiel with his feathered wheels within wheels. Or Isaiah eating a book. Or Jeremiah breaking his pot. Or Balaam's talking donkey. What do we make of these? The author Eugenia Price was moved to consider Christ because Ezekiel's absurd wheels caught her imagination. She saw Scripture pulsate. In Scripture's paradoxes we find the fundamental dualities and tensions involved in being human. Scripture is the whole onion, with layers and layers of meaning to unpeel. There is plenty for our right brain to play with.

To get ready to pray, then, we should not endlessly read devotional books. Rather we should allow our imaginations freedom as we read the Bible, with study guides if necessary. Then our prayers will show the shine and sparkle of Scripture.

In fact, we could use a prayer from Scripture and apply it phrase by phrase to ourselves or to the person we're praying for.

Take, for example, Paul's prayer in Ephesians 1:15-21:

> Ever since I heard about your faith in the Lord Jesus and your love for all the saints, I have not stopped giving thanks for you, remembering you in my prayers. I keep asking that the God of our Lord Jesus Christ, the glorious Father, may give you the Spirit of wisdom and revelation, so that you may know him better. I pray also that the eyes of your heart may be enlightened in order that you may know the hope to which he has called you, the riches of his glorious inheritance in the saints, and his incomparably great power for us who believe. That power is like the working of his mighty strength, which he exerted in Christ when he raised him from the dead and seated him at his right hand in the heavenly realms, far above all rule and authority, power and dominion, and every title that can be given, not only in the present age but also in the one to come.

Can I apply this prayer from Scripture phrase by phrase? What is the "hope of his calling" for me? How will that affect what I leave undone this week? What is "the riches of the glory of his inheritance" as I try to figure out how to pay the dentist? What is "the exceeding greatness of his power" as I wrestle with a rebellious teenager?

When we have friends far away whose needs are hard to picture—missionaries, for example—using a Bible prayer like this to guide our thoughts can help. Here are other such prayers:

Ephesians 3:14-21
Colossians 1:9-14
Philippians 1:3-6, 9-11
2 Thessalonians 1:3-4, 11-12
The Lord's Prayer (Matthew 6:9-13)

Sometimes a simple request or exclamation can become

the backbone of a pithy prayer. John Wesley did this with the plea "Forgive me":[6]

> Forgive them all, O Lord:
> our sins of omission and our sins of commission;
> the sins of our youth and the sins of our riper years;
> the sins of our souls and the sins of our bodies;
> our secret and our more open sins;
> our sins of ignorance and surprise,
> and our more deliberate and presumptuous sin;
> the sins we have done to please ourselves,
> and the sins we have done to please others;
> the sins we know and remember,
> and the sins we have forgotten;
> the sins we have striven to hide from others
> and the sins by which we have made others offend;
> forgive them, O Lord, forgive them all for his sake,
> who died for our sins and rose for our justification,
> and now stands at thy right hand to make intercession
> for us, Jesus Christ our Lord.

Sometimes just for my own private journal, not for publication, I find it stretching to pray using a single biblical theme:

> Today I see I'm wearing matching socks:
>   His mercies endure forever.
> I drove internationally to Vancouver and back without
>   trouble even though I'd lost my driver's license:
>   His mercies endure forever.
> Joel took the initiative in creative play today:
>   His mercies endure forever.
> Among seventy new adult students, there are many
>   stimulating questions and new worlds:
>   His mercies endure forever.
> Rick has lost thirty lbs.:
>   His mercies endure forever.
> Today Joe called, Mark called, Sharon wrote:
>   His mercies endure forever.
> At thirty-nine, on research days I can still go to work
>   in running shoes, jeans, and a Chinese jacket:
>   His mercies endure forever.

SINGING: SPIRIT-FILLED PRAYER

Scripture is intimately connected with prayer. So is singing. Paul writes that we are not to be drunk with wine (or other excesses we women indulge in), but in place of that we should be filled with the Spirit, bursting out in snatches of psalms and hymns and spiritual songs, singing and making melody in our hearts to the Lord. As a public prayer, singing also is ministry. What we sing in the kitchen affects our children and our guests.

My dad is a preacher's son. Once I asked him, "Dad, was it your father's preaching that brought you to Christ?"

"No," he said thoughtfully, "I think it was more my mother's singing."

In singing, as in Bible study and prayer, we touch hands with other Christians across time and space. We remember friends with whom we have sung certain songs. We remember former churches and fellowship groups. We may also think about the life of the songwriters.

Take the hymn "Children of the Heavenly Father." Who wrote that? Lina Sandell. When? Her family was migrating from Sweden to America, when a fierce storm blew up. Battling the elements, Lina's father was swept over the side of the ship and drowned. Lina faced a strange continent, an alien life— and now suddenly she was without a father. We touch base with her faith when we sing the words she wrote then:

> Children of the heavenly Father
> Safely in his bosom gather;
> Nestling bird nor star in heaven
> Such a refuge e'er was given.

> God his own doth tend and nourish,
> In his holy courts they flourish;
> From all evil things he spares them
> In his mighty arms he bears them.

> Neither life nor death shall ever
> From the Lord his children sever;

At the will of your Defender
Every foeman must surrender.

Though he giveth or he taketh
God his children ne'er forsaketh;
His the loving purpose solely
to preserve them pure and holy.

More secure is no one ever
Than the loved ones of the Savior;
Not yon star on high abiding
Nor the bird in homenest hiding.[7]

PRAYER: AN AGENT FOR CHANGE IN SOCIETY

Finally, prayer leads to action. Prayer skimpily grounded in Scripture may contain beautiful thoughts, but they are often in a fog, divorced from real life. Scripture-immersed prayers have a sense of the reality of time. The generations of mankind are going somewhere, and we are contributing to that march. As T. S. Eliot has said, in Christianity the timeless enters time and redeems it from insignificance.[8] Because Joshua meditated on the Word, on the ongoing story of God's interactions with people, he not only had channeled prayers, he also had relevant action. He came out of his closet to help shape society.

We shape society first by the power of prayer itself. Prayer focuses God's grace holistically. There are times when we're blocked on the human level. People refuse to talk things out. But that need not stifle us. We can talk things up. By prayer, we channel God's grace to those we love. In prayer we fight against the powers of darkness which threaten our corner of the world. Through prayer we struggle on the world's behalf. We tap God's resources and let them pour toward our neighbors. Prayer also helps us see people more holistically.

The universe is not set. Through prayer as well as through action, we can become co-laborers with God, molding contemporary events. If this is so, how much more we have a responsibility to know what's happening in the world—to pray with the Bible in one hand and with the newspaper in the other.

PRAYER: AN AGENT FOR BLESSING

But there is more. As we ask God's blessing on a friend or on parts of society, we, like Joshua, sometimes discover ways to *be* that blessing. Public prayer is one way. Over the phone with a troubled friend. Over a coffee cup with a neighbor. Over a skinned knee or a disputed toy with children. Over a mangled computer printout with a colleague. Would you dare? How awkward—the first time, anyway. But why not let the power of God invade our relationships?

Prayers said with the eyes open can be channels of blessing too. In the Old Testament and the New Testament we read beautiful greetings and leavetakings—which really are prayers:

> Grace be unto you, and peace, from God our Father and from the Lord Jesus Christ. I thank my God upon every remembrance of you, always in every prayer of mine for you all making request with joy, for your fellowship in the gospel from the first day until now; being confident of this very thing, that he which hath begun a good work in you will perform it until the day of Jesus Christ (Philippians 1:2-6 KJV).

> The LORD bless you and keep you; the LORD make his face shine upon you and be gracious to you; the LORD turn his face toward you and give you peace (Numbers 6:24-26).

One missionary in West Africa says that such rich hellos and goodbyes still characterize many of his Muslim neighbors. So much so that missionaries might use greetings as a chief channel for communicating Christian truth to many Muslim peoples.[9]

The Muslims have a concept, *baraka*, that parallels the Hebrew concept *shalom*. It means wholeness, health, blessing, fullness. Why not fill our hellos and farewells with *baraka*, with *shalom*, with the well-rounded grace of God tailored to the needs of the individual we are with—as did so many in the Old Testament and in the New Testament.

This implies walking around aware of the needs and hopes of those we're with—and aware of God's blessing in relation to those needs and hopes. It means "seeing no man after the flesh" (2 Corinthians 5:16 KJV), "regarding no one from a worldly point of view," but as Christ regards him. It means "always being prepared to give an answer to everyone who asks you to give the reason for the hope that you have" (1 Peter 3:15), an answer applied to our friend's hopes and dreams.

Betty Mae is a friend who models some of this active blessing through greeting. With a big house, high standards, lots of guests, volunteer and committee responsibilities, and two children, Betty Mae focuses quietly on me whenever I visit her, and I believe she does the same for each person. "What have you been learning?" she asks over a cup of tea. "How have you been growing? Where are you struggling? What are you dreaming? How are your relationships? Your work?" By her active, thoughtful, and specific greetings, Betty Mae blesses many.

AN ALTERNATE REALITY

In prayer, channeled by Scripture, we tap into an alternate reality. We don't flip out to a separate reality. We join it to this world. We make it accessible for others. We open the faucet of God's order, God's blessings, and let them shower here.

Let's not pretend to a false spirituality that does nobody any good. Let's be honest. We do have to slog through Januarys. We do fear, and doubt, and freeze up. On the other hand, let's admit the other side: we each have experienced God's love at our points of need.

The prophet Jeremiah went through his January of the spirit when nobody would take him seriously and his work seemed useless. Finally, fed up with the long hours, the risks, and the low benefits of prophesying, he resigned. He quit. He said, "I'm burned out."

But he hadn't calculated on the renewable energy of God's Word. It wasn't long before Jeremiah changed his tune. "If I say, 'I will not mention him or speak any more in his name,' his word is in my heart like a fire, a fire shut up in my bones. I am weary of holding it in; indeed, I cannot" (Jeremiah 20:9).

Jeremiah's meditation on God propelled him back into the world. God's Word was fire in his bones.

It isn't enough to know what's right. Beyond that, we need energy and courage to do what's right. We need motivation. That comes as we let ourselves be filled with God's Word, like Jeremiah. As we wait upon the Lord, praying over his Word day by day, our spirits are renewed and we soar up like eagles (even if we work with turkeys!). Instead of gritting our teeth and plodding on, we fly.

Martin Luther King tapped into that alternate reality through prayer. He discovered his first speech for a mass rally while he was praying. The evening of that rally he had twenty minutes in which to prepare. Pressures pounded. Most important, How could he electrify people for positive action yet defuse their hate? Were these goals irreconcilable? Nearly half of that twenty minutes King spent praying. Then the words flowed from his pen into his outline: "I Have a Dream. . . ." His philosophy was born. The Civil Rights Movement of the 1960s marched in nonviolently.

Through prayer we become not dropouts, and not conformists, but creative deviants. We become a saving remnant. People of conviction in the middle of the mass. Salt of the earth.

God knows how desperately the systems of this world need to be plugged into an alternate way of living. I let my mind skip from situation to situation, country to country—conditions that look hopeless, the crud that has piled up over eons of despair. Yet, in place after place, a saving remnant creates. Where whole mountain ranges have been denuded, a saving remnant replants forests. Where people have been brutalized and dehumanized, a saving remnant organizes communities where people discover hope, identify their problems, utilize available resources, help each other, and develop whole lives. Where children are left lonely by careerist parents, a saving remnant stokes cozy homes that warm the neighborhood.

Lighting our candles at God's fire, day by day, gives us the power to be this saving remnant which the world needs so desperately.

What have you come to the kingdom for? we have asked. We are to "seek first the kingdom." Yet even that may become an idol. I find that even when I've chosen my priorities well, even when I'm working hard in a ministry, it's so easy to focus on projects rather than people. On law rather than grace. On structure rather than freedom. On the kingdom rather than the King.

Whether in public or in private, then, we busy women need prayer. As A. W. Tozer has put it, "We are called to an everlasting preoccupation with God, to be worshippers first and workers only second. . . . The work of a worshipper will have eternity in it."[10]

Sisters, we are loved. God's warmth has thawed our Januarys. God's Word has sizzled fire in our bones. Therefore, we've come to feel the creation mandate and the love mandate so strongly that we cannot rest.

1. Author Unknown. Quoted in a sermon heard in Hong Kong in 1968.

2. Some of the references in this paragraph were first brought to my attention in a book by John Stott, *Your Mind Matters* (Downers Grove, Ill.: InterVarsity Press, 1973).

3. Leticia Magalit, *How to Lead Bible Studies* (Manila: Inter-Varsity Christian Fellowship of the Philippines, 1972). Used with her permission.

4. Bernard Ramm, *Protestant Biblical Interpretation* (Grand Rapids, Mich.: Baker Book House, 1970), passim.

5. Blaise Pascal, *Pensées* (New York: Random House, 1950), pp. 363-365.

6. John Wesley, "Forgive Me," in *Eerdmans Book of Famous Prayers*, ed. Veronica Zundel (Grand Rapids, Mich.: Eerdmans, 1984), p. 63.

7. Lina Sandell (1832-1903), "Children of the Heavenly Father."

8. Richard Ellman, "T. S. Eliot," in *Masters of British Literature*, Vol. II (Boston: Houghton Mifflin), p. 987.

9. Larry Lenning, *Blessing in Mosque and Mission* (Pasadena, Calif.: William Carey Library, 1980).

10. A. W. Tozer, *Gems from Tozer* (Harrisburg, Penn.: Christian Publications, Inc., 1979), pp. 13, 15.

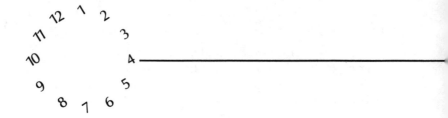

7

SHARING CHILDREN

How to Nurture
Your Child's Caregiver

H ere I perch, in a cubicle of a public bathroom. My post-pregnant tummy folds comfortably on my thighs. I have just delivered a paper at a conference. Copies were grabbed up. I was lionized. There was talk about my being a main speaker next year. Meanwhile, I sit here, bra hanging from a hook, other clothes draped over a bar, and pump my breasts.

First comes a watery substance like coconut milk. Then glorious rich white milk. A pity to tip it in the toilet. My neighbor has her whole freezer stocked with her milk in case she ever goes anywhere. That's not for me. I don't want to bother about sterile equipment. Baby Michael does fine on occasional formula: He's seventeen pounds at two-and-a-half months.

Someone enters the next stall. Embarrassment. Squeak! The rubber ring in the pump protests as I move it up and down, up and down. What must she think? She washes her hands. Click! Her lipstick is opened. Rip! She pulls out a towel. The door opens, she taps out, the door shudders and clangs shut. Blessed privacy in which to carry on my desperate self-emptying.

My baby was not scheduled, but my work was—including three distant conferences the first five weeks after Michael was born. What to do? For eighteen dollars I bought a Marshall pump, the next best thing to an electric pump. I traveled, conferred, pumped—and seven days later came back with more milk than ever.

Why bother with all this?

Because the love of Christ constrains me. Because God's gifts to me must be expressed. I have a responsibility to my baby; I also have a responsibility to the larger world. The two are not mutually exclusive. In fact, women have been coping with multiple responsibilities for a long time.

How? In many cases, by sharing their children with other responsible and caring adults who like children and want to be involved in family life. "Babies are an inestimable blessing and bother," as Mark Twain so aptly put it. In America many a mother experiences both within the privacy of the four walls of her home. But such blessing and bother can be more evenly distributed. They *are* more evenly distributed in many parts of the world. Our own ancestors did not huddle in isolated nuclear families, but shared many childraising hours with kin, neighbors, and helpers. Sharing children can benefit everyone. And it can enable all of us to serve more holistically, with all our hearts and souls and strength and minds.

As I described in Chapter One, my doctor shocked me when he announced I had to go immediately to the hospital for the delivery of our first baby. I panicked. Suddenly I wasn't ready. We had had time to exercise our gifts in dominion to God's world. We had had energy to be ambassadors of God's revelation of himself in the Lord Jesus. Why had we complicated everything by bringing a new person into that battle?

Certainly with her family a mother could exercise dominion and be an ambassador of the Lord Jesus. But could she do it in a wider sphere? I discovered she could. Along the way, though, I've had to learn some coping strategies. This chapter explores one.

I will be suggesting that we need to develop slightly different models of childsharing—that is, less compartmentalization between childless and childblessed people; among grandparents, parents, and teens; among men and women. We need to develop models whereby the responsibilities—and the rights—to be significant role models, disciplinarians, and trainers for children can be more broadly shared.

The child himself needs to know who his parents are, who has ultimate responsibility and authority. But he also needs other adults to play a significant role in his life. Recognizing that, we can network those relationships for our children.

EXPANDING THE CIRCLE OF CAREGIVERS

In the early 1970s I lived for four years in the Philippines. My husband studied in the Asian Center at the University of the Philippines, and I directed publications for the Philippine Inter-Varsity Christian Fellowship. While there, I learned some new things about family life. Now, as I watch friends struggling to be adequate parents in the traditional U.S. nuclear family setting, and as I have children of my own, I feel impelled to describe some of the richness of Filipino families.[1]

What did I see?

A whole cadre of committed caregivers circling each child. One version of the extended family at work. As we Americans cultivate our family extensions, we may learn something from such arrangements.

Strong women. In the Philippines, I discoverd strong women. Not stronger than men, but strong. Later I found this was typical of Southeast Asian women. Psychologist George Guthrie has described such women:

There is a remarkable equality of sexes in Philippine society. Women occupy important positions in government, industry, and business. Within the family, the woman usually controls the finances. In many cases in all economic classes she earns as much as half of the family income. Inheritance is equal without regard to age or sex, a tradition that goes back to pre-Spanish times. Long after he has become an adult, a son will seek his mother's advice or may receive her unsolicited opinions on a large number of matters. In spite of this there do not appear any particular difficulties with what we call masculine protest in women. The society is not ambivalent in this matter; the woman's place is in the home and in the market, the office, and the rice field too. Women with families of six to ten children carry full time jobs of great responsibility while their children are raised by relatives, maids and older siblings, and nobody feels rejected or disapproves.[2]

Relatives. Filipino women are strong partly because Filipinos emphasize both husband's and wife's relatives equally. This means that women are links to power and wealth just as much as men are.[3] We Americans, too, would emphasize both husband's and wife's relatives—if we paid attention to relatives at all. But we focus on the nuclear family. Unlike us, it is said that the average Filipino has 400 relatives. Beyond that are "adopted kin": Every wedding, every birth, is an opportunity to joyfully link up with more friends as adopted aunts and uncles.

Emphasizing kin and emphasizing both sides means a huge pool of potential babysitters. In one famous study of mothers in six cultures, it was found that the Philippine community had the greatest number of people generally who interacted on a level of intimacy.[4] Filipinos have learned to value as togetherness what we might consider crowding or stifling. As for domestic cooperation among women, again Filipinos showed the closest ties. The reason given was that "here the kin group is often bilateral, and a women has her own relatives as well as her husband's close at hand."[5]

Children valued. All these people wouldn't necessarily be an asset to a harried mother—except that small children are prized. Caring for them is a joy. Small Filipino children grow up with constant human attention. But this certainly does not all come from mother. It comes from teenage aunties, grandmas, or hired helpers, who may live in the home. Or from neighbors or regular visitors.

Men and women. I have mentioned aunties, grandmas—but fathers and even uncles are expected to do their stint at childcare, too.[6] Last week, for example, I attended a Filipino church party here in Seattle. The mother and father who invited me both were active in singing and dancing. Who took care of their ten-month-old baby girl? Two uncles, in their late teens and early twenties. As a matter of fact, as soon as I stepped into the picnic grounds my own baby was taken from me and cared for with delight while I ate, socialized, and mingled.

Sibling care. In my years in the islands I got to know my landlord's daughter during the period in which she had her fifth and sixth children. A typical "strong woman," she held a government administrative position on her island. She managed a home and small hacienda. Simultaneously, she pursued a Ph.D. program at the University of the Philippines on a different island. I used to watch her children, ages ten to one, playing for hours without any squabbles or sibling rivalry, adjusting the games to make it possible for the little ones to join in at varying levels of skill. It was expected that the older ones would take care of the younger ones, and children were trained that way.

This was reinforced by the names Filipino brothers and sisters would call each other. Instead of using given names, younger siblings would call out "Older sister!" or "Older brother!" With every call they would be reminded of their different obligations to each other.

115

Such ties continue into middle age. A forty year old will help his or her twenty-five-year-old sibling financially, in housing, in connections, in advocacy. He can never wash his hands of his brother. On the other hand, when the older person requests a service, the younger sibling must drop everything and come running gladly.

Though this system has its disadvantages, it does build strong interpersonal ties. No one is left lonely. Everyone has a place and a people.

By contrast, in my own American family, we sisters were raised to achieve independently. When I returned from the Philippines I had new eyes for my sisters, and a new sense of relatedness with them. Now I'm making my sons' sense of brotherliness and mutual caring and concern a priority—above table manners, music lessons, academic excellence, and sports competence.

People, not things. "In what country are the children raised like birds, made to sleep in caged-in beds, and love their dolls more than their parents?" This question is raised by Khamsing Srinawk, writing in *Bangkok Magazine* about his U.S. tour. He suggests that, whereas we Americans are concerned to surround our children with good toys and learning activities, Southeast Asians are concerned to surround their children with good people.[7]

As in Thailand, children in the Philippines grow up in a world where privacy is not valued. A baby spends most of his hours in physical contact with somebody. When unhappy, he is fed. The baby is the center of diffused, loving, indulgent attention, in contrast to more specific and focused attention that American babies receive. He is not pushed. He is protected; if he is ready to crawl into any potential danger, he is picked up and carried off. He has few toys, but lots of children to play with. He is carried around to all areas of adult life, not kept home on a rigid schedule. Consequently, he does not live in the American child's make-believe world. It is suggested that this babyhood experience nurtures an extremely sociable child who is more people-oriented than thing-oriented, who is somewhat passive toward exploring his environment, and who is not particularly inclined toward strict schedules.

Such children may learn to care a great deal for people. They may learn unselfishness, courtesy, and grace. On the other hand, they may also learn conformity. They may be less self-reliant than Americans. How important is that? Each of us must decide.

Is it possible, however, that our American children could be enriched by an expanded circle of caregivers as much as they are by a circle of toys?

Stable, happy mothers. For mothers, what are the implications of this childraising context? The study of six cultures found:

> Tarong (Filipino) mothers are medium in their expression of warmth and are emotionally stable. They spend relatively little time caring for their children. . . . The most unusual characteristics of the Tarong mothers are their emotional stability and extent to which others help them with their childcare. The hypothesis presented concerning the origins of these factors assumes that these two characteristics are functionally related; that is, the emotional stability of this group of mothers is due, in part, to the presence of other adults who can help them care for children.[8]

We American mothers could use that kind of help, too. So we would be smart to cultivate networks of mutual commitment with senior citizens, singles, teens, or others who would like a child in their lives now and then. Some singles and senior citizens have other priorities; let's give them our blessing and let them go in peace. But for others, a child can introduce them to a new dimension of living, a new world. Nuclear families are great for cultivating individual personalities; but let's not shrivel up in our nuclear families unduly. Let's ponder people like the Filipinos and see what we can learn from them.

After glimpsing such diffuse childcare in the Philippines, I settled back into life in the U.S. Now I have three sons. They electrify my days. But from their conceptions the priority was not decorating the nursery so much as it was locating warm, capable mother substitutes.

How to Nurture Your Child's Caregiver

How do you find such a person? There are many ways. An exchange with neighbors, friends, or other mothers in your church. Regular days with grandma or an auntie—even an adopted one. All kinds of daycare. I once found an excellent childcarer through a classified ad that she placed. Pray, ask friends—and eventually the Lord will provide what you need. That is no pious truism. He cares for you—in this very area.

What do you look for? A good caregiver will:

Radiate love, common sense, and a quick ability to
   solve practical problems.
Ensure the children's safety.
Discipline when a child is defiant, hurts, or repeatedly
   annoys another.
Encourage the children to create things they enjoy
   making.
Introduce new and varied play ideas appropriate for
   the children's ages.
Monitor the children's fulfillment of their
   responsibilities.
Keep the place picked up.

Who can find such a virtuous woman (or man)? Remember, the one who cares for your child is not a finished product when she arrives. She (or he) is not a machine. She is a person, capable of growth. She needs to grow. You can nurture her. Of course you want to hire the very best. On the other hand, you may want to balance that with your desire to employ someone who needs a job. In any case, look for someone who has potential for growth. Someone who has gifts and interest in childcare, and particularly in your children.

One study showed that the most important quality of a caregiver or mother substitute was an irrational commitment to the child. In other words, love. You can't buy this. But keep it in mind during your initial interviews and your early trial period. You may even want to discuss this with your caregiver, and ask what level of commitment she's prepared to have.

In return, you must give more than money. Here are four areas in which to do that: consider her a professional, consider her a person, consider her family, and consider her unique strengths.

CONSIDER HER A PROFESSIONAL

If your caregiver is young, she may see herself moving pizzas from freezer to oven to table, playing with the kids, keeping peace, managing naps and bedtime. If she's older, cleanliness, discipline, and plentiful food may be a big part of her agenda. In either case, with your enthusiasm and specific suggestions, you can move her from a mellow caretaker to a dynamic nurturer. If she is loving and sensible and interested in developing her gifts with children, she can be trained.

Although at first she may see herself as a passive babysitter, you can change that. Continually reinforce how important, challenging, and complex her role is. Build her up as a skilled manager. To do this:

Share child development materials with her. Get a book or two on the characteristics of children at the ages of yours. Tell her you want her to read certain sections. Give the impression that you assume she'll be delighted to grow here. Then discuss the characteristics, pick her brain, seek to learn together about children. "Iron sharpeneth iron; so a man sharpeneth . . . his friend." (Proverbs 27:17 KJV). Become friends in the care of your children.

At the very beginning, go over the above characteristics of a good caregiver with her. Some points must be discussed in detail. What are the children's regular responsibilities? What are they not allowed? What discipline methods do you use? Does she feel comfortable with these? Are there any unsafe features at your place (or her place)? Is a given child attracted to certain dangerous habits right now? What does each child especially enjoy doing right now?

Provide her with a challenging repertoire of activities, resources to do them, and possibly even behavioral development goals. Develop

119

lists, cards, or files—and accompanying supplies such as colored paper, boxes of puzzles, craft and sports boxes.

In what areas might your child develop?

- Large muscle activities—outdoors and indoors
- Fine muscle activities—arts and crafts, blocks, Legos, clay, all kinds of paper creations
- Imagination—book stories, made-up stories, dress-up dramas, play with dolls, small figures, cars
- Music and poetry—from pot-and-pan bands to making cassette tapes
- Physical projects—cooking, gross carpentry, papier-mâché, pet care, plant care
- Social skills with various ages
- Spiritual and ethical discernment
- Boredom battlers—Counting some group of items, imitating various steps, face contortions, sounds; make up rhymes; think of opposites; add episodes to a spur-of-the-moment story

Explain that you would like your caregiver to aim for a balanced variety of such activities. Periodically review the week's activities, and ask for her input.

A child raised in this context won't want much TV. He won't bicker and fight so much either. He'll be too busy being creative and having fun.

For all this, pay her as well as you can. Many a once-a-week "auntie" doesn't want pay. You must compensate her in other ways. But if she's working to earn money, don't try to see how little you can pay her. Rather, try to see how much you can possibly afford. Presumably she is with your children because that is an expression of her gifts. You are away from them in order to express some of yours. Is there any reason why you should earn substantially more than she does?

CONSIDER HER A PERSON

Remember her on her birthday, at Christmas, possibly even on Mother's Day. Give her fresh flowers once in a while. Or other little things such as you would like . . . perfume, jewelry, concert tickets, a book. Teach your children to respect her, to be thoughtful of her and to give her small gifts.

Pray for her. In order to do that helpfully, ask about the various areas of her life without being nosy. Listen well. In return, share some of your own struggles and joys. If she is a Christian—or even if she's not—you might occasionally pray with her. If she prays, ask her to pray for you.

On a lighter level, *trade shopping tips. Exchange used items.*

Assume that your relationship will continue even after her employment ends. Make some effort to keep in touch. This will teach your child that people are not things to be used and discarded. People are not disposable. Human relations are valuable. Loyalty matters. In this regard, give an occasional thought to your caretaker's future. In Chapter Four we glimpsed Betty Mae Dyck, a Canadian homemaker who lived several years in the Philippines. Betty Mae developed good long-term relationships with her maids. After each of these young women had been with her for a few years, she pondered their gifts and interests in relation to their possible future. Then she helped them on to their next stage. One became a professional seamstress. Some went to Bible School, some to business school, some married. In each case, she helped them get set up.

Build a foundation for her future. You may not be able to help much financially, but you might help a great deal by assessing your caregiver's gifts, asking "stretching" questions, encouraging her, connecting her with opportunities, writing references, and speaking up for her.

CONSIDER HER FAMILY

Frequently ask her how her various family members are doing, and make the sacrifice of taking time to listen. Visit her home once in a while if she babysits in yours. Give her a chance to be hostess, to be in charge. Expose yourself to the insecurity of being on her turf. This is how a reciprocal relationship develops. It is good for your children, too, to see her in her own context.

As well, welcome her family to occasional dinners or other social events at your place.

Not only my childcarers but also their families have brought richness to my children. In their early years, my boys spent mornings in two other homes. In each case my children were the only nonfamily members. Both mothers grew up in large, happy families where home was the center of love and fun, work and social networking. Baking, gardening, quiltmaking, arts and crafts—my boys have been involved in such areas far beyond my competence or interest. In each case, my childcarers' husbands delighted in their children, and occasionally would go to work late or come home early in order to spend time with the kids. My boys benefited from these dads' woodworking and roughhousing and stories. Today if I were looking for a childcarer, I would naturally gravitate to a member of a large family for whom home has been an orderly but diversified hub of many activities.

CONSIDER HER UNIQUE

June, one of my childcarers, excelled in preschool activities. During the first half of each morning she concentrated on the babies, while the four year olds—hers and mine—had free play. Then the babies went down for naps and June helped the four year olds explore some new project. Money was tight, so construction paper and popsicle sticks served many uses. We still have June's cut-out freestyle drawings of the three billy goats gruff, the troll, and the bridges. Also the three little pigs, the wood, straw, and brick houses, and the wolf. In our minds are the stories—verbatim—and the songs: "Who's Afraid of the Big Bad Wolf?" and so on.

When June moved, I was determined not to settle for less. But Margaret turned out to have other gifts. A superb infant-carer, gourmet cook, and house manager, she had a *laissez-faire* attitude to preschool activities. I had to accept this, and to make up the difference by letting her do more of my cooking and myself struggling with the arts and crafts, which are not exactly my natural medium. The point is, people are not interchangeable. Each childcarer is unique. A caregiver is a person. So you must adjust to her, just as she does to you. Encourage her strengths: you will get the best results because she will be doing what she is created to do.

Beyond professional childcarers, other unique friends can bless and be blessed by our children. Let's not forget aunties and uncles, adopted or biological. Anne Sorley is a professional woman who has played a key role in her nephews' and nieces' lives. They visit her for week-long vacations. Together, she and her nephew have learned to fish. She has been the one he has turned to with questions about God, love, life and death, poverty and suffering. His mother has encouraged this: she believes the children are not given to her and her husband alone, but to the larger family. When Anne's nephew turned eleven, she—whose business involved international travel—took him to Haiti with her for two weeks. Although this involved considerable expense and inconvenience, Anne found it a delight to introduce him to the larger world, and to share in his reactions. When his sister turned eleven, Anne took her to Haiti for two weeks, too. "The trips were life-changing experiences for all of us," Anne says.

Gladys Petersen is an editor who has been involved with her nephews similarly. Although she is handicapped by deafness, and is overweight, she enjoys outdoor adventures in new places. As her nephews have entered their teens, she has taken each on a special vacation. One chose a week in Hawaii—sailing, snorkeling, scuba diving, surfboarding, climbing mountains, exploring cultures. Another nephew joined Gladys for a white water raft trip down the Colorado River. These are highlights not only of the boys' lives but also of Gladys's life.

Who would you trust to share the highlights of your children's lives? Let's not overlook singles. They experience peripheralization in many of our churches. Yet, like Anne and Gladys, they can be complementary role models for the children of the church—children of single parents as well as children of two-parent families.

THE RISK OF BIRTH

God will honor our efforts to achieve this balance. In her book *The Missionary Wife and Her Work,* Joy Tuggy acknowledges many stresses that plague harried mothers overseas. But she goes on to give these encouraging principles:

- A woman's first and only responsibility is to fulfill the Lord's will for her personally. This is ascertained in a daily walk with him.
- Her ministry can be greatly enlarged, under God's direction, by marriage and motherhood.
- Since these relationships are from the hand of God, they do not conflict with the mission work given a mother; on the other hand, they do direct it along different channels for a period of years.
- The peculiar responsibilities for child-rearing occupy only a comparatively brief part of a missionary mother's time of service, while both she and the work benefit permanently from her years under the discipline of motherhood.

Tuggy adds: "If a woman has an urge to make Christ known, all her life, however she is occupied, will be missionary life."[9]

Mothering and professional work do not need to be either/or. The isolated mother and child in the nuclear family home have certain richnesses. But taken to extremes, this is neither God's ideal nor the human norm.

Unfortunately, many mothers who have small children, but who are burning to express their gifts, bear their children—pop, pop—and grit their teeth for the seven years or so till the children start school. How sad to rush through our childbearing marking time as though there were something greater ahead. When my son says to me—

"Can you still be my mommy when I'm a fireman?"

"Mommy, when you grow down and be a little boy, you can sit in the back seat."

"Did Daddy have a beard when he was married? Well, did he have a chin?"

"Can tennis shoes run faster than feet?"

"Carlo can't go to hell, because he's allergic to smoke."

—there's very little that I accomplish professionally that gives me more satisfaction. I'm in no hurry to see the last of my preschoolers. I'm glad I don't have to choose between them and creative expression. Admittedly, I'm fortunate that I can make a small income while expressing my gifts and service professionally. Tough is the lot of the mother who must earn, yet whose gifts lie elsewhere. Still, most gifts taken generally— gifts of expressiveness, encouragement, listening, assertiveness, pragmatic problem-solving, management, adaptability— can be honed in a variety of contexts.

Of course we can't have it all. Mothers, above all, know this. Therefore, we ask prioritizing questions. We say no—in order to say yes. We dare to take risks, to start things, only because God's love experienced daily turns us on.

In addition, a mix of activities, if not overdone, will keep us healthier: "Women who have three roles—paid employment, marriage, and parenting—have the best general health status, the lowest morbidity, least long-term disability and restricted activity, and the lowest incidence of drug use," comments Lois M. Verbrugge, Ph.D., of the University of Michigan School of Public Health. A news brief in *Baby Talk* magazine, August, 1981, reported this. "Dr. Verbrugge analyzed national Health Interview Study tabulations as well as a study of the health of 412 women in Detroit," the news brief explains. "Both social selection and social causation may explain the health of working mothers. 'Only the healthiest women can manage several roles,' Dr. Verbrugge said. 'On the other hand, multiple roles give women several sources of satisfaction, and this may be a powerful determinant of their good health.'"[10]

To enrich our children, to enable people with caregiving gifts to use those gifts, to enable *us* to use *our* unique gifts, and to bless God's larger world, we must cultivate other adults who can play a significant role in our children's lives. We must network those relationships.

Parenting is scary, especially if you take your work in the

world seriously. But it's not impossible. Expanding the circle of caregivers helps. When, right before Christmas, I fearfully delivered my first son to the world, his birth announcement, a poem borrowed from Madeleine L'Engle, underlined the risky life to which we parents—and all Christians—are called:

The Risk of Birth

This is no time for a child to be born
With the earth betrayed by war and hate
And a comet slashing the sky to warn
That time runs out and the sun burns late.

That was no time for a child to be born
In a land in the crushing grip of Rome;
Honour and truth were trampled by scorn—
Yet here did the Saviour make his home.

When is the time for love to be born?
The inn is full on planet earth,
And by a comet the sky is torn—
Yet Love still takes the risk of birth.[11]

1. Of course, there are disadvantages to the Filipino arrangement. There is less opportunity to cultivate individual uniqueness, there is less articulation of personal feelings, there is gossip and offended feelings and smoldering resentments and occasional explosions and feuds. There is less adult focusing on an individual child, one-to-one. Nevertheless, there is also much worth considering.

2. George Guthries, *ix Perspectives on the Philippines* (Manila: Bookmark Press, 1968), pp. 72-73. See also this comment by Fred Eggan, "Philippine Social Structure," Ibid., p. 30:

> In the Philippines there is about as great a degree of equality between men and women, between husbands and wives, as exists anywhere. In most areas in the Philippines, except in those areas where there has been very strong Spanish influence, the husband and wife are essentially a mutually cooperating pair. The husband, for village purposes, is the head of the family, and whatever position and prestige the husband has in the community the wife has too. He may be obeyed in public, but the wife normally controls the family purse strings, carries out the economic activities, and is in charge of the household and children. In fact, in a number of cases the woman

in the family may have more prestige than the husband. Usually, however, the two are pretty well balanced, with their roles designed to be complementary, cooperative, and fairly equal in status.

3. This Philippine kinship structure—a bilateral kinship structure—is unlike the unilateral structures of the Chinese, Japanese, Vietnamese, Middle Easterners, and some Africans. In traditional, precolonial times, the equality nurtured by the Philippine structure meant that women enjoyed many rights—to independent acquisition and transmission of property; to initiate divorce; to speak in councils; and to govern.

4. Leigh Minturn and William Lambert, *Mothers of Six Cultures: Antecedents of Child Rearing* (New York: Wiley, 1964), pp. 209, 220.

5. Ibid.

6. For examples see Thomas Kiefer, *The Tausaug: Violence and Law in a Philippine Moslem Society* (New York: Holt, Rinehart, and Winston, 1972), pp. 33, 46; or, Edward Dozier, *The Kalinga of Northern Luzon* (New York: Holt, Rinehart and Winston, 1967), p. 27.

7. Khamsing Srinawk comments:

> It is almost correct to say that Thais and Americans are differentiated from birth. Thai children live with their parents until they marry. An infant sleeps in his parents' room and learns to sit or stand on his parents' laps. Before he can walk, he is carried by his parents or his brothers and sisters. Grandparents shower him with attention. The family tie in Thailand is strong, meaningful.

> In the United States I have noticed that children are sometimes raised on formulas and objects. Thai children are motivated to love their parents: in the U.S. children love and attach themselves to toys. Thai children sleep on a cushion the size of a pillow, so they can be carried about, or in a hammock beside their parents. American children sleep in caged-in beds in a room of their own. When a Thai baby cries he gets an immediate response; in America a child may cry until he falls asleep again. I don't intend to say which system is better, only that we are being formed differently.

> While visiting a good friend of mine and his family during the early part of my stay in America, I thought that they raised their child as one raises a bird. Occasionally the child was allowed to come out of his room to toddle about, completely on his own whether he stumbled or fell. When the time was up he would be sent back to his caged-bed. He was supposed to sleep.

> Later, when I had met more people, I began to realize that way my friend raised his child made sense in context.

> His child will grow up in an industrialized society where life depends more on material things than it does in a country like Thailand.

8. Minturn and Lambert.

9. Joy Tuggy, *The Missionary Wife and Her Work* (Chicago, Ill.: Moody Press, 1966).

10. Lois Verbrugge, quoted in a news item in *Baby Talk*, August 1981.

11. Madeleine L'Engle, "The Risk of Birth," reprinted from *A Widening Light: Poems of the Incarnation*. Edited by Luci Shaw. By permission of Harold Shaw Publishers, Box 567, Wheaton, IL 60189, ©1984 Luci Shaw.

TRAINING CHILDREN FOR THE BATTLE

"Why Can't Jesus Be Superman?"

While I sliced cheese for sandwiches, three-year-old Daniel tumbled through a somersault on the couch. Then his eyes peered at me over the furry brown top.

"Why can't Jesus be Superman?" he asked.

"Jesus is strongest," I answered, knife in midair. "He made—"

"But why didn't he shoot the bad guys that nailed him to the cross?"

Violent role models. How do we cope with them? Why can't Jesus be Superman?

We can begin by agreeing with our children. They sense that life is a battle. We can say: "You're right!" Starting with the trivial conflicts that hold them enthralled, we can lead them to the true struggle. We can teach them we *are* in a battle—for the kingdom of God.

What are our weapons? The commissions we've explored in this book: exercising dominion and being ambassadors of God's love. Mothers have responsibilities to fulfill these commissions like everybody else. But mothers must do more. We must pass the torch.

Of course we would rather protect our families from the sweat and wounds of battle. But the family that tunes out the problems of the world around it, the family that focuses on itself, loses its significance. We must reach out. We must be Esthers for our families, plugging them into the risky larger world. Why? Because God has called us to exercise dominion. Because he has commissioned us to be his ambassadors of reconciliation. And because our children are aware that life is battle: Unless we introduce them to the true struggle, they will spend their energies in second-rate fights.

THE FAMILY IS TOP PRIORITY

To be sure, we need to take time to create a sheltered oasis in our homes. We need to withdraw and be quiet with our families. Mothering demands our best. The family is not on a level with political involvement or social service or church work or any other institution. Here I take issue with some Christian mission executives. When a new family applies to be missionaries, but insist they want to educate or raise their children in some particular way, I have heard mission executives comment to each other, "Where has all the dedication gone?"

And they quote J. Grant Howard's *Balancing Life's Demands*:

The family is not more important or less important than other relationships. It is just as important as the church, the job, and your other relationships. . . . Some will no doubt plead for the priority of the family because it started way back in Genesis, long before the church and human government. Doesn't that make the family more important? No, chronology does not necessarily imply superiority. The world and work came before the family in Genesis. That doesn't make them more important. Heaven comes last on God's timetable. That doesn't make it less important.[1]

Such an attitude has helped shape our own ideals, unfortunately. Many outstanding Christian leaders have not been outstanding parents. Take, for example, Jonathan Goforth, one of the greatest missionary evangelists to China in the late 1800s.

"Rose, I've developed a new strategy," Jonathan said to his wife one day around the turn of the century. "You see these population centers here, and here—" he jabbed at a map, "and here? No witness to Jesus in any of them. Listen: Here's my idea. You know how God has blessed our ministry. Thousands have responded. So—what do you say we travel this next term? Establish a base for a month, preach in the surrounding area, then move on. Establish another base in a center. And so on."

Historian Ruth Tucker continues the story:

As Rosalind listened, her "heart went like lead." The idea itself was impressive, but it simply was not suited to a family man. Exposing their little ones to the infectious diseases that were so prevalent out in the villages was too risky, and she could not forget the "four little graves" they had already left behind on Chinese soil. Although Rosalind initially objected, Goforth went ahead with his plan, convinced it was God's will.[2]

Sure enough, they left behind another little grave. Five of their children died.

William Carey and David Livingston had severe family problems too. These men are Christian heroes. When we think of the faith of our fathers, we think of people like these. They have shaped our evangelical Christian ideals. Their views of women and the family have affected us. Yet we can learn from them not only what to do, but also what *not* to do. We are challenged to work at family relationships which don't contradict the love of Christ we talk about.

HOME IS WHERE THEY HAVE TO TAKE YOU IN

The family is *not* on a level with other institutions. It is wrong to say it is. The family is for love. Whether your team wins or loses, whether your job is making or breaking it, the family is where you can be cared for. Hugs. Trivial comforts. Secure routines. "Love is the giving of unearned gifts in gratitude for life together," says sociologist Gibson Winters. And the family is for love. When so much of our life is rationalized, streamlined, and planned, we desperately need some sphere in which people are irrationally committed to us, not for what they can get out of us, but just because.

In our work and classes and other associations we are known partially and in fragments, but at home there is the possibility of being known wholly. What you do on Saturday morning as well as Saturday night. Your checkbook. Your closet. Your parents and grandparents. The hours you keep. Your snacks. The family knows you from a lot of angles. There's more possibility to know you as a whole person. That, too, is why the family supersedes other groups.

Is that our experience today, given fragmented urban life? Maybe your family is not loving. Maybe it's a conglomeration of strangers. Modern compartmentalization has invaded the family. Is home becoming just a fast food stop between meetings?

Still, family life still retains more potential for wholeness than any other structure. Human homes began when God observed that it was not good for man to live alone. Man was made to live in a community of meaning. So God gave his blessing to the family. Friends love you. Sometimes the church loves you. Colleagues may care deeply. But over the long haul, the family endures. "Home is the place where, when you have to go there, they have to take you in," as Robert Frost observed.[3]

The family is not equal to any other institution. It's at the heart of all our connections.

Therefore, mothering demands our best.

Paradoxically, the family that focuses on itself loses its significance. There is a good side to those mission executives' protests. A family focus can be selfish. Must a child have a Walkman? A personal computer? Private schooling, and private lessons? Or even just a bike?—before we parents can give time and money to the work of the Lord?

Early on, we parents must model dedication to larger causes. Kingdom causes. Beyond love, this is what children need most. Especially if we can involve them at their level.

BEING ESTHERS FOR OUR FAMILIES

In *Growing Up in Christ*, a guide for families of adolescents, Eugene Peterson writes, "The task of the parent . . . is not directly to confront the problems of the young and find the best solutions to them. It is to confront life, and Christ in life, and deal with that. A parent's main job is not to be a parent but to be a person."[4] Our job is to model exercising dominion, like Laura in her pregnancy counseling centers; to model being an ambassador of God's love, as we visit immigrants.

In her article "Reclaiming Motherhood for a Restless Culture," Gladys Hunt writes,

> We've been to blame every time we have glorified a role instead of insisting that a person's wholeness must give substance to that role. That principle is true whether the individual is an executive, a waitress, a preacher, or a doorman. God wants whole people who live holy lives. Whether their title is Mother or something else, he is looking for wholeness.[5]

In other words, mothering is not enough. A mother must be a person in her own right, with space for her creativity and commitments.

Alta Barge Shenk was such a mother, in spite of being isolated as a missionary in rural Africa. She modeled for her children a wholeness that I envy:

> As adults it was clear to us that Mother was on a journey . . . We were astonished at the joyousness and contemporaneity of her faith. Although our parents had buried themselves in the backwoods of Africa, as it were, she was modern, understanding, sympathetic, and perceptive of the issues that we confronted in our university experiences, or in city ghettos, or in modern suburban culture. . . . She was walking with God in response to the call of Jesus Christ.[6]

Children need to see mothers modeling the use of their gifts in service. This way they learn about the larger world. They learn about choices. They learn about priorities. Temple Gairdner's "Prayer Before His Marriage" is one that those of us who are old-fashioned American moms need to pray daily with regard to our children:

> That I may come near to her
> Draw me nearer to You than to her.
> That I may know her
> Make me to know you more than her.
> That I may love her
> With the love of a perfectly whole heart,
> Cause me to love You more than her and most of all.[7]

The family that concentrates on itself loses a lot. We need to be Esthers for our families, stretching them, connecting them to God's larger world.

A few years ago I conducted an orientation workshop for a team of Christian medics headed to a refugee camp in Somalia.

"Today Mommy's going to teach a class to some people who are going to Somalia," I explained that morning as I zipped Dan's pants and tied his shoes and brushed his hair.

"What's Somalia?"

"A country where there are many troubles. A war—"

"Are there soldiers?"

"Umhmm."

"Are they killing people?"

"Umhmm. And the people run away; they leave their homes and stores and gardens. Now they have no food. So Mommy's class is going to take food to the poor people in Somalia. And Mommy is going to teach them how to do it better."

Daniel ducked the hairbrush. Then he popped up on my other side. "Mom," he said, "can we invite Somalia to our house?"

Children need to be plugged into God's larger world.

WHY CAN'T JESUS BE SUPERMAN?

How do we teach our children about kingdom battles?

First, by talking about real struggles in the world today. Children suspect that life is a battle, and they grope toward a theology that makes sense of this. "Why can't Jesus be Superman?" three-year-old Daniel asked while he tumbled on the couch and I sliced cheese for sandwiches. "And why couldn't he shoot the bad guys that nailed him to the cross?"

Why indeed? Lunch preparation would have to go on the back burner while I applied my mind elsewhere. Daniel and his friends love to grab "capes" out of the clean towel bin and charge around the yard—or sail off the furniture if they get a chance— yelling "Superman!" Violent role models captivate them. Though we monitor TV, we find that He-Man, She-Ra, Thundercats, Silverhawks, and Star Wars characters seep into Dan's consciousness from many sides. He is enthralled. Maybe this is a modern version of the macho cowboy image. Maybe it is a by-product of raising children to be confident, assertive, self-reliant individualists in the American mold.

But does Jesus come in a poor second?

We can campaign against too much media violence; but we can't be ostriches. Violence is a part of life. In Daniel's Bible story book is a two-page picture of Abraham with his knife raised above Isaac. I find it in poor taste. But it is Scripture. As is the picture and story of the crucifixion of our Lord. Aggressiveness exists. Not only that: Jesus submitted to it. How do we explain this? And how do we discuss violence with our small children?

We can teach them that we *are* in a battle—for the kingdom of God. Hunger: We hate it. We donate cans to food banks. Ignorance of the Lord Jesus: We hate it. We support missions. Our own sinful habits: we hate them, and ask the Holy Spirit to help us hack them down.

Of course we may be wrong when we identify enemies. So we gear up humbly. We're willing to change. We keep listening for God's direction, and for the wise counsel of others. But we can't sit on our hands. Right doctrine is not enough. Knowledge must be expressed in action. We can teach our children this. Our agressive impulses are not something to be repressed. They are there for a purpose: to be directed against evil. If we interpret evil as powers rather than as people—powers inside us, too—we can learn (and eventually teach) a lot through "imprecatory Psalms," for example.

Children deserve to know where the true battle lies.

This past month, twelve years into our marriage, Michael and I have been fumbling toward a will. He scratches decisions on a pad of paper, while I scrub the pots and pans. But we've crashed into an impasse: guardians for the children.

"Susie and Gene live such a natural life in such a wholesome out-doorsy environment," I say wistfully. "The kids would learn how to cope with their environment, how to become self-reliant . . ."

"But Rod and Linda are right where the action is—"

"—the urban jungle. That pit! Rapes in schools. Drugs. Concrete. Neon. Cruising. Hollywood. No roots," I object.

"What sort of Christian life would they learn from Susie and Gene though? They're so laid back," Michael argues.

"That doesn't mean they don't have a deep quiet faith," I persist.

"But no sense of battle! Rod and Linda are in the thick of things; they're shining lights mingling with pushers and runaways and occultists as well as media and computer people. I want my kids to be actively involved in the struggle to conquer the powers of darkness with the light of Jesus Christ. . . ."

Children of battle: Shaping a will has dragged Michael's dream out of the closet.

We are wrong if we withdraw to TV football and Bible studies and potlucks and bowling, and sing "This World Is Not My Home." This world is the Lord's. He loves it. We are to struggle for his dominion, his reign over his own property and people.

Second, we can teach our children to identify with the victims. Jesus did. Too often we smear pancake makeup over our wounds. We screen out of our consciousness the painful picture of friends who have been tortured by cancer. We repress the memories of our own dark night of the soul. But the Bible bluntly reminds us that we "who were dead in trespasses and sins" have been enlivened. The Bible repeatedly told God's people to remember their forty years in the wilderness and to tell their children about them. As we share our own wounds it will nudge our children—and will remind us—to identify more with victims, rather than with those who have it made.

"People with more means can afford the luxury of allowing their sons to live in a world of fantasy, of only seeing the good side of life, of protecting them from bad companions and obscene language, of not hurting their sensibilities by witnessing scenes of brutality, of having all their expenses paid for them," says a poor Mexican boy in Oscar Lewis's modern classic,

The Children of Sanchez. "But," he continues, "they live with their eyes closed and are naive in every sense of the word."

Real pain and violence—not just TV caricatures—are all around us. People in developing countries, even people in U.S. ethnic churches, shield their children much less. The children learn about abortions and stabbings and abuse not from the media but in context, where adults can interpret it.

One way to teach children to identify with victims is by launching off a current news event. Since Michael and I have discussed the plight of Guatemalan Indians with Daniel, he and his dad sometimes zoom around the yard, towel-capes flying, yelling—not "Batman!" but—"Catch the landgrabbers!"

Relating familiar institutions to the world scene also teaches him.

"Let's go to McDonald's Mommy! I want to go to McDonald's! Can we go to McDonald's?" Daniel clamors from time to time.

But he's learned that we pace our visits not because we don't have money—that would be a lie—but because we choose to give part of our money to poor children who never get any hamburgers.

Third, we can teach our children self-control in quarrels. ("At last she gets to what matters," some parents will sigh. But we should see backyard disputes in the context of our total attitude to violence.)

"That's mine!"

"I'm playing with it!"

"Let me see—"

"I had it first!"

"Give it—"

"No!"

Scuffle. Plop. Thud. "Yeowww!"

What happens when the bad guy erupts right in our own play yards?

140

In this tussle, Carlo and Daniel agreed to submit to a timer: each child could have the toy for five minutes. For half an hour I set and reset the bell. By the second full exchange, however, relinquishing the toy man was becoming automatic at the sound of the gong.

Children need to learn to negotiate. Later it will pay off in marriage, in business.

To teach self-control, we also can introduce positive role models for dealing with aggressors.

"If Jesus can't shoot the bad guys, can he ask the policeman to do it?" Daniel asked, the day after we discussed Jesus' death. So we talked about the basis for law and order, the place of human structures in God's plan, and humane treatment of suspects.

But what happens after prison? Charles Colson's Prison Fellowship newsletter provides bedtime stories. Now they are being enacted in Lego play. And live: "Dad, will you come out and play Charles Colson with me?"

Eventually, difficult as it is at an age when one makes absolute good/bad distinctions, Daniel must come to understand that all of us are sinners, just as we are all made in God's image.

"Why didn't Jesus shoot the bad guys who were nailing him to the cross?"

"Because he loves even the bad guys. Just as I love you. Even when you're very bad I wouldn't shoot you, would I? In fact, sometimes you are a bad guy. Sometimes even I'm a bad guy. When I get grouchy and grab things without asking. Do I do that sometimes?"

And we talk about how Jesus went to the party of that "landgrabber," Zacchaeus, and helped him change. Some evening soon I'll dazzle Daniel with a word picture of Jesus as he is described in Revelation 1—golden, eyes flaming, voice booming like Niagara falls, holding seven stars, and zapping everything in sight with a sword, with a force that makes Darth Vader pale into insignificance. Jesus endured, not passively,

141

but for the joy, the victory ahead. We, too, dare not pass our time in quiet resignation. God commissions us to live heartily, as to the Lord, to live abundantly, to do whatever our hand finds to do with all our might. True, Jesus is lamb as well as lion. He is a wounded healer. He is a scandal to the macho strong defense creed of the Western world. Yet, like a butterfly, his waiting yields wings, new life, creativity. His death and resurrection take the inevitability out of history.

He is our model.

SUNBATHING WHILE THE WORLD BURNS

We women perhaps are not raised with a sufficient consciousness of battle. So we sunbathe while the world burns. Yet when we live this way we deny Christ's Lordship over that world. Of course there is a time to create a tranquil oasis where our family and friends can be refreshed. But there is also a time to march. And when we march we will encounter and have to decide what to do about the neighbor lying by the side of the road.

What about our children? If we abhor war, it is not enough to teach our children to sublimate their competitive instincts through sports. There is a real battle. As we ourselves enlist in the struggle for Christ and his kingdom, we can channel their energies too. Children may be too young to

> march in the infantry
> ride in the cavalry
> shoot the artillery

but certainly they can serve in the Lord's army.

Remember Catherine Booth, co-founder of the Salvation Army? She modeled battle for her children. All eight of them followed her into the fray, as Christian leaders.

Like Catherine, let's commission our children for battle as we put on our own helmets and gear. Let's pray for them:

Now may the radical justice of God the Father,
the liberating forgiveness of God the Son,
and the revolutionary transforming presence of God
   the Holy Spirit
so blow through your lives
that you may go forth into this broken world
and fight the Lamb's war
knowing that the risen King has already won
the victory over injustice, violence, and death.
Hallelujah. Amen.[8]

Portions of this chapter originally appeared in "Mommie, Why Can't Jesus Be Superman?": How to Discuss Violence with Your Pre-schooler—and Get a New Perspective on Christ's Sufferings," *Christian Herald*, May 1982.

1. J. Grant Howard, *Balancing Life's Demands* (Portland, Oregon: Multnomah Press, 1983), p. 89-90.
2. For details on the lives of Jonathan and Rosalind Goforth see:
   (1) Rosalind Goforth, *Climbing: Memories of a Missionary's Wife* (Chicago: Moody Press).
   (2) Ruth Tucker, *From Jerusalem to Irian Jaya: A Biographical History of Christian Missions* (Grand Rapids, Mich.: Zondervan, 1983) pp. 189-93.
   (3) J. Herbert Kane, *Life and Work on the Mission Field* (Grand Rapids, Mich.: Baker Book House, 1980), p. 175.
3. Along the same line, a humorous observation with some deep truths comes from anthropologist David Schneider:

Performance in a friend is everything, for there is nothing else. A good friend is one who executes the tasks of loyalty with skill and courage and dispatch. A good friend is there in time of need, and does not bumble the job. And a good friend is dropped for failing. . . . Friendship combines the advantages of freedom to evaluate performance and terminate the relationship with the requirements of diffuse solidarity, which do not specify exactly what a friend has to do. Friends are relatives who can be ditched if necessary, and relatives are friends who are with you through thick and thin whether you like it or not. . . . You can really count on your relatives.

It is this, of course, which makes sense of the phrase that a man's best friend is his dog. . . . A dog, just because you can demand the highest standards of loyalty, of diffuse solidarity, is a kind of friend . . . and the diffuse solidarity occurs in a context where you can get rid of the dog if you want to.

David Schneider, *American Kinship*, (Englewood Cliffs, N.J.: Prentice-Hall, 1968), p. 54.

4. Eugene Peterson, *Growing Up in Christ: A Guide for Families with Adolescents* (Atlanta, Ga.: John Knox Press, 1976), p. 15.

5. Gladys Hunt, "Reclaiming Motherhood for a Restless Culture," *Christianity Today*, 2 May 1980.

6. Elaine Sommers Rich, *Mennonite Women: A Story of God's Faithfulness 1683-1983* (Scottdale, Penn.: Herald Press, 1983), p. 146.

7. Temple Gairdner, "Prayer Before His Marriage," *Book of Famous Prayers*, (Chicago, Ill.: Eerdmans) p. 68.

8. Ronald Sider, *Christ and Violence* (Scottdale, Penn.: Herald Press, 1979), p. 101. Used by permission.

9

FAITH OF
OUR MOTHERS

Role Models

On her shoulder, Mary Slessor carried her adopted baby. Clinging to her skirt was her five year old, and with her right hand she coaxed along her three year old. Two older children sloshed behind. Sloshed, because they were trudging through a mangrove swamp in West Africa. It was night, for their boat had reached its destination late. They could not see any snakes that might lie across the path or drape from trees above. But they could hear leopards. To keep the big cats at bay, Mary belted out hymns. The children chimed in. "Our singing would discourage any self-respecting leopard," Mary wrote to a friend later. On this night no other adult was within miles.

Because no missionary had the time or, perhaps, the courage to go, Mary Slessor and her children were moving in to live with the fierce Oyokyong people in what is now Nigeria. The year was 1888.

Today we women are faced with multiple role possibilities and we struggle with our identities: What are my priorities? What dare I do? How assertive should I be? In this quest, Mary Slessor is a worthy addition to our gallery of role models.

Unafraid to Risk

Mary was born in 1848 in Scotland. Population had boomed in the early 1800s. Crops, however, had failed. On the non-agricultural front, the steam engine was squelching cottage industries. Desperate for jobs, families migrated to cities. Many lived, begged, and died on the streets. The Slessor family of nine lived in one room.

Mary's father was a shoemaker, and her mother a weaver who earned ten shillings a week for fifty-eight hours of labor. Because weaving required nimble fingers more than strength, and because a woman's wage was nearly half a man's—and a child's wage only one-fourth—there was almost no work for men in weaving mills. Boys could work until they became men; then they were sacked. In this grim setting, and after three of the children died, Mary's father became an alcoholic. On payday Saturday nights he would bluster in, ready for violence or sex, small children notwithstanding. To protect her mother, Mary many times drew his anger to herself.

One wonders what Mother Slessor thought of God's goodness when—on top of marital loneliness, beatings, the inevitable squabbles of children cooped up in one room, children's sicknesses that led so quickly to death, and nearly sixty hours of work outside the home every week—she waddled after her fifth, sixth, and seventh pregnancies to the stone-cold communal bucket outhouse located beside the manure heap.

In fact, we know what she thought. A speaker had captured her imagination, and she dreamed that one of her sons would be a missionary to West Africa. So she checked the *Missionary Record* out of the church library and read missionary stories to her brood. She encouraged them to "play missionary."

Yet all her sons died.

Was that the end of a dream? No. Mary stepped forward. Her sisters were horrified. "Can't you volunteer to go to some safer field, like Jamaica or India?" they begged. But Mother Slessor was thrilled.

Out of this background Mary Slessor went to West Africa to become known among Africans as *Eka Kupkpro Owo*, "the mother of all the peoples." As James Buchan observes in his excellent biography, *The Expendable Mary Slessor*, "The squalor, the poverty, and the hunger of a Scottish slum taught her how to share the squalor, the poverty, and the hunger of the West Africa of her day."[1]

What did Mary find in that new continent? Two centuries earlier, before the slave trade with the West, the people of Calabar had lived in self-governing villages. Economically they had specialized: fishing villages traded with farmers, pottery villages traded with canoe makers, blacksmith communities traded with weavers.

Big-time slave trading exploded this simple lifestyle, according to Buchan:

> The West African tribes soon realized that to trade in human beings was the way to power and wealth and those which did not have an anchorage already migrated to the coast and occupied one. . . .

> As the trade developed and they needed more warriors and more labour the coastal tribes began to keep back more and more of the captives for their own use. A small House, slave and free, could number up to a thousand. But a large one, like those of the Calabar towns, owned thousands of slaves and hundreds of trading and war canoes. . . .

> Between 1720 and 1830 about a million slaves were
> shipped out of Calabar, while thousands more died
> in the anchorage or were butchered there. The
> chiefs grew accustomed to looking on human beings
> simply as merchandise. But because they shared the
> same human life, the cheapening of the lives of the
> sold cheapened the lives of the sellers . . . . By the
> beginning of the nineteenth century, Calabar life
> . . . was a squalid travesty of what it had once
> been. . . .[2]

Life was cheap. Torture was imaginative. Slaves, women,
and children especially were expendable. Here Mary stepped
in. Besides preaching, teaching, and nursing, she rescued
women and hundreds of babies thrown into the jungle. Rarely
did she have fewer than a dozen such children living in her
makeshift house. During one period, each infant was sus-
pended in a cradle hammock made from a wooden crate. Tying
a string to each crate, Mary would lie in bed at night and pull
strings as each baby needed soothing. To bathe her babies,
Mary put four big milk cans on the stove to warm the water,
plopped in four babies, pulled them out and dried them, plopped in four more—all the time discussing points of African
law with those who sought an audience with her.

As we have noted, Mary's knowledge of indigenous law
eventually propelled her into being the first woman vice consul
of the British Empire. This knowledge was gleaned as she lived
"not only like an African, but like a poor African"—in native
houses, sleeping beside big, sweating, native bodies, eating
native food, going barefoot, suffering local diseases—but
awake, aware, curious, asking questions, categorizing information, applying it.

Mary's participation in local councils could be feisty. A
British government officer remembers, when an African
showed up who had been forbidden to come to court because
he had been rude:

> Suddenly she jumped up with an angry growl, her
> shawl fell off, the baby (which had been on her lap)

was hurriedly transferred to somebody qualified to hold it, and with a few trenchant words she made for the doors where a hulking overdressed native stood. In a moment she seized him by the scruff of the neck, boxed his ears, and hustled him out into the yard, telling him quite explicitly what would happen to him if he came back again without her consent. . . . Then as suddenly as it had arisen the tornado subsided, and (lace shawl, baby and all) she was gently swaying in her (rocking) chair again.[3]

In spite of unorthodox methods, Mary's genuineness, courage, and true concern made her welcome at councils.

LIBERATED BY THE WORD AND THE SPIRIT

Mary Slessor was not the only tough Anglo-Saxon Mary in the West African jungle in those years, however. Mary Kingsley, intrepid explorer, journalist, naturalist, amateur anthropologist, and society's darling, also trekked through. When she recounted her perilous exploits in *Travels in West Africa* and other books, and in articles such as those that appeared in *The Spectator*, she became an acknowledged African authority.

Kingsley came in velvet hat, buttoned up jacket, and knee-high boots. Slessor had long since discarded the Victorian missionary's hat, gloves, boots, bustle, long curls—and sometimes even her dress. Kingsley secreted a revolver and dagger in her clothes. Slessor went unarmed. Kingsley was glamorous. Slessor, due to malaria, looked scrawny and washed-out. Nevertheless, when Kingsley came to visit Slessor, the two took an immediate liking to each other, and they continued to correspond for the rest of their lives.

Both Marys modeled the strong, creative woman. Fashionable Kingsley, however, was subordinated to the scientific philosophy of the day. Slessor was subordinated to the Word and Spirit of God. Because of this, poorly educated Mary Slessor was liberated to have broader views and a much wider impact for justice and wholeness than Mary Kingsley.

Social Darwinism was widely believed in the latter quarter of the nineteenth century. Races were ranked on an evolutionary scale. Mary Kingsley swallowed this.[4] Mary Slessor, however, was not bound by contemporary scientific philosophy. She took her marching orders from the gospel. For her, every slack-mouthed slave was made in God's image and was someone for whom Christ died. It was never inconvenient, then, to go rushing off—in the middle of the night or with a full agenda or in the middle of a malaria attack—to rescue one more insignificant, threatened person.

Of Mary Slessor, Mary Kingsley said,

> This very wonderful lady('s) . . . abilities, both physical and intellectual, have given her among the savage tribes a unique position and won her among many, white and black, a profound esteem. Her knowledge of the native, his language, his ways of thought, his diseases, his difficulties, and all that is his, is extraordinary, and the amount of good she has done no man can fully estimate. . . . This instance of what one white can do would give many lessons in West Coast administration and development. Only the type of man Miss Slessor represents is rare . . . Miss Slessor stands alone." [5]

How assertive should we be? Mary Slessor offers one model. In Mary we see how a fairly ordinary woman was liberated beyond the philosophies of her day and set afire by the Word and the Spirit.

A CLOUD OF WITNESSES

When you read about Mary, though, how do you feel? Inspired? Or, on the other hand, intimidated? There's no way that *I* would go through leopards and pythons at night. Even so, I need to fill my mind with strong role models like Mary, however partially her modeling applies to me. All around me are consumer-oriented women. I can so easily get bogged down. I must balance the vision of reality which the media nurtures with a gallery of role models like Mary, a cloud of witnesses—both historic and contemporary—who show me what an ordinary woman can do when she stretches.

Actually, Mary was not unique. Many strong women have gone before us. In this chapter I'll give glimpses of women who have enriched me. *You* ought to compile your own gallery of role models. Every heritage embraces an army of strong sisters. We need to get acquainted.

ACROSS TIME: EIGHTEEN CHILDREN, NO MAN, NO HOME

Apart from mission fields and far cultures, stretching and daring have characterized pioneer women in our own heritage. Many of our own foremothers resemble Proverbs 31's virtuous woman—buying and selling land, importing and exporting goods, manufacturing textiles—more than they resemble us with our vision snagged on the unmowed front lawn. In *Mennonite Women: A Story of God's Faithfulness 1683-1983*, Elaine Sommers Rich describes such creative women:

> From (their) early years in America, Mennonite women have received a fourfold heritage: (1) learning to work with their hands, (2) practicing hospitality toward kinfolk and strangers, (3) being frugal, and (4) contributing to the welfare of the community in a spirit of cooperation. They were co-partners with their men as transmitters of these values.[6]

These women raised vegetables to sell at weekly farmer's markets. Some peddled butter, eggs, and coffee cakes door to door. They cured meat, made cheese, dried apples, boiled sap, made soap, raised chickens, preserved berries. "In the winter they had bees, schnitzing bees, butchering bees, quilting bees, and even rag bees, when they got together to tear mat rags."[7] Some canned one thousand quarts of food a year. In the early days of this country, when over half of the children born did not grow up, these quarts sometimes made the difference.

I think of Veronica Ulrich Eberly. Born in Switzerland in 1685, she and her husband Heinrich decided to emigrate to the New World. They had six children ages one to twelve. Together they made their way to Rotterdam, to the ship *James Goodwill*. Heinrich, however, returned home to get something—and the ship sailed without him.

> One can only imagine the anguish of the young mother with her family . . . as the grim reality of her situation weighed down upon her. Through all the journey and for many months and years she probably lived on the hope that he would follow in a later ship and one day they would be reunited. But the months and years passed by, and Veronica never heard of Heinrich again.[8]

Veronica and her six children settled in Lancaster County, Pennsylvania. Movers unloaded her scanty house furniture under a big oak tree, and left. The nearest neighbors were two miles away. They were Indians. Here this woman exercised her mind to subdue God's earth. She raised a flourishing family which has many descendants today.

I think of Barbara Osch, who migrated from Germany in 1824. She and her husband Johannes developed a prosperous two-hundred-acre farm in Ontario, produced seventeen children, and gave leadership in the church. But Johannes, "only fifty-six, father of eight sons, decided to move again. So Johannes, Barbara (pregnant with her eighteenth child), the young children, and their earthly possessions on several wagons followed the Huron Road west. . . .

"A year later, on March 12, 1859, suddenly, unexpectedly, Johannes died of a ruptured appendix . . . Barbara and her children completed the family house and tilled the land."[9]

I think of Susanna Brunk. She was born a sixth child. Her mother died. Her stepmother did not care for her, so she spent her teen years as a hired girl in other people's houses and fields.

In 1859, however, she married Henry Brunk, and in 1860 gave birth to Johnny. Life was looking up.

Then the Civil War exploded. As a conscientious objector, Henry was imprisoned. He deserted from his work crew and had to hide out—sometimes in the attic, sometimes far away.

Baby Sarah arrived on September 17, 1862. Less than two months later—Susanna alone at the deathbed—Johnny died. The father attended the funeral, but had to act like a stranger and leave during the last hymn, for scouts at the funeral were searching for him to put him into the rebel army.

In the next eight years, Susanna bore five more children. Then the family moved West, to Kansas. But Henry fell sick. When they finally arrived on their land, Henry

> unharnessed his horses, turned them to graze on the prairie, went to bed under a crude board-wigwam shelter, and never got up again, succumbing to typhoid fever after eight days.

> Susanna—age thirty-four, eight months pregnant—had six young children, all sick, and no roof to cover their heads. Henry C. Jr. was born on December 6, just thirty-six days after his father's death. Thirteen days later five-year-old Fanny died of typhoid. Just before the little girl died, she reached upward with a look of joy on her face. Another three days and the oldest girl, Sarah, died. In the spring the baby died.

> Now Susanna had four children, ages two, four, six, and eight. George R. Brunk, the two-year-old, said in later years that among his first memories was a glimpse of his mother standing by the table in their one-room cottage, crying as she was cutting her husband's clothing into garments for her two little boys. A few years later her son Joseph's left arm had to be amputated just below the elbow as a result of an accident.[10]

We squirm when we compare what these women faced with what we face. A little history, and suddenly being a "football widow" doesn't seem nearly so bad! Susanna, Barbara, Veronica, and unnumbered others rose to the challenge. And often they felt a certain fulfillment in being strong enough to "make do." These women didn't shrivel up. They created order. With the chaos around them, they exercised dominion. They transmitted hope. As they rested in the Lord, they found their strength renewed.

ACROSS SPACE:
TENS OF THOUSANDS OF BIBLE WOMEN

"Bible women" have been the unsung grass roots heroes of the church around the world, according to historian Ruth Tucker. She refers not to volunteers, but to salaried professionals, paid first by missions and later by local churches. Tens of thousands of such Bible women have slipped nonthreateningly into women's quarters, as well as being welcomed into the limelight of community centers. They have evangelized. They have discipled. They have accompanied and trained new Western missionaries. They have sung and performed dramas. Many have received theological training equal to a pastor's. Others, on the other hand, have been illiterates who have memorized much of the Bible. Tucker says:

> 'Together, the Western missionary woman and her indigenous counterpart, the Bible Woman, were responsible for a major share of the evangelism and Bible teaching that brought to birth the churches of the non-Western world.' This has been particularly true in China in recent decades. Arthur Glasser during his trip to the Far East in 1981, found that 'fully 85% of the leaders of house churches thriving in the People's Republic of China are women.' It may be that Bible women—this vast army of lowly, often-forgotten and unrecognized women—have contributed more to the cause of world evangelism than any other group of Christian workers.[11]

Evelyn Quema, at the time of interviewing a few years ago—was twenty-four years old, short, stout, single, and a minister of the gospel. She was hardly noticeable in a crowd of Filipinas her age. Yet in three years she had planted four churches, had seen two hundred solid conversions to Christ and several hundred more which she had not been able to follow up; had developed five hundred student contacts who had attended Christian meetings at least three times; and had taught thousands of children and youth.

As a high school student, Evelyn showed a great gift in witnessing to her faith. Thirty of her personal relatives were brought to faith in Christ. All nine of her brothers and sisters, as well as her parents, were drawn by her testimony. But she did not want to be a minister. As the oldest child, she wanted to help her family financially. She hoped to be a lawyer or a doctor.

However, she felt a clear call from God. So she enrolled in Bible school. Then, at the age of twenty-two, she found herself sent to the city of Baguio. She had six dollars, which was to last her a month. She had no contacts, no place to live, no building for a church. Her assignment: Start a church, make it self-supporting as soon as possible, and start branch churches.

She arrived in town (with her mother) on Thursday. She rented a building on Friday. She invited people in the market on Saturday. She conducted a service for thirty on Sunday, and saw four conversions. Within a few months her congregation was self-supporting.

In three years she started twelve regular Bible classes for children, eleven outstations, (one, five hours away by bus where she spent five days of each month), and four regular churches.

To those who disagree doctrinally regarding women preachers Evelyn says, "I would never have been a Christian if a woman hadn't brought the gospel to me."[12]

Beyond the tens of thousands of paid Bible women, there are of course millions of unpaid women of the Bible. Today the church around the world displays some strong sisterhoods. Sometimes I wonder if they shame us by comparison. The Women of the Good News in Zaire and Central African Republic, for example, include many more than thirty thousand women. They meet weekly in groups for Bible study, with rotating leadership. They memorize booklets of Bible verses.

Annually, they sponsor a Day of Prayer, a Women's Rally Sunday, and a four-day district conference. Every two years they have leadership training seminars for key women who are selected by their local groups. Beyond this,

> Each group is subdivided into as many as five smaller groups that carry out different outreach assignments: visiting the sick (providing water, food, wood, and words of witness and encouragement), evangelizing unbelievers, ministering to those who have left the church fellowship, maintaining church building and grounds, and visiting the elderly.[13]

In the city of Beni, the Women of the Good News "carry out a wide variety of services, with evangelism as a primary emphasis. They visit new mothers at the hospital, bringing them clothing for the baby; they do home repair for poor widows; they bring food to prisoners; and they fund scholarships for Bible school tuition."[14]

When did you last do a home repair for a poor widow? Aren't there single mothers right on your street who need that kind of help? Knowing about these sisters across the globe challenges us.

BEYOND SPIRITUALITY: A FIXED TIME SLOT FOR THE POOR

And what more can I say? For time would fail me to tell of the powerful women who have graced so many ages and places. One more group stand out in my memory, though: Evangelical Anglicans in Victorian England.

For a period of time, helping the poor became fashionable among dedicated Christians. Prisons; better conditions for prostitutes, deprived children, mentally ill; reform of the factory system; improved housing . . . Are these topics for our coffee breaks today? Yet there was a period in British history when Christian women raced to get involved in such efforts. They volunteered in societies like the Female Mission to the Fallen, the London Female Preventive and Reformative Institution, the Friendly Female Society for the Relief of Single Women of Good Character, the City of London Truss Society, and the Institute for the Cure of Various Diseases by Bandages and Compression. Their "ragged schools" not only educated poor children, but also found jobs for those who finished. They believed, as Hannah More put it, that comfortable women ought to "*set aside a fixed portion of their time as sacred to the poor.*" It was as natural and as popular as enrolling in an aerobics class is today.[15]

THEY DARED

In tradition after tradition we find role models. In our own growing years, too, we've all known women of grace. For me, Edna, Anita, Melba, Marj. When I'm inclined to be lazy or timid, I consciously call these old friends to mind. I savor them. I bask in their fire.

We ought to acquaint ourselves with foremothers and sisters who stimulate us to stretch as they demonstrate what is beautiful and strong.

That doesn't mean idolizing them. Take Mary Slessor. She had her faults. She was bossy and cranky with co-workers. She was not a team player. Her theology was rudimentary, as were her teaching methods. So what else is new? Of course she had her weaknesses. Because of these very limits her witness hits close to home. In Mary, as in other foremothers, we see what a fairly common woman can do who dares to be strong. Who dares to be creative. Who dares to blaze.

1. James Buchan, *The Expendable Mary Slessor* (New York: Seabury Press, 1981), p. 7.
2. Ibid., pp. 35-36.
3. Ibid., p. 146.
4. Missiologist Jon Bonk documents this in his article "All Things to All Persons: The Missionary as Racist-Imperialist 1860-1918," *Missiology* (July 1980). Therefore, Kingsley could write, "The difference between the African race and the white (is not) . . . a difference in degree, but a difference in kind. . . . The African is analogous to the (dodo) bird in being, like him, a very early type, whom Nature, in her short-sighted way, has adapted to the local environments, with

no eye on (the) future." As well, according to Bonk, Kingsley was "irked by (missionaries') willful ignorance as to the true nature of the African mind, which manifested itself in the 'difficulty (they experience) in regarding the African as anything but a Man and a Brother' and in the misguidedly dogmatic conviction of 'the spiritual equality of all colors of Christians.'"

5. Buchan, p. 148.

6. Elaine Sommers Rich, *Mennonite Women: A Story of God's Faithfulness 1683-1983*, (Scottsdale, Penn.: Herald Press, 1983), p. 35.

7. Ibid., p. 35.

8. Ibid., p. 31.

9. Ibid., p. 59.

10. Ibid., pp. 67-68.

11. Frances Hiebert, "Missionary Women as Models in the Cross-Cultural Context," *Missiology*, October 1982, pp. 455-460 as cited by Ruth Tucker, "The Role of Bible Women in World Evangelism," *Missiology*, April 1985, p. 144.

12. James Montgomery, *New Testament Fire in the Philippines* (Manila: Church Growth Research in the Philippines, 1972).

13. Ruth Tucker, "African Women's Movement Finds Massive Response," *Evangelical Missions Quarterly*, July 1986, p. 286.

14. Ibid., p. 286.

15. Ian Bradley, *The Call to Seriousness: The Evangelical Impact on the Victorians* (New York: Macmillan, 1975), pp. 122-24.

10

BURNING OUT

What Kind of Old Woman Will You Be?

In my mind I've already laid the first brush stroke toward a picture of the woman I would wish myself to be in the twilight of my life. I see an old woman walking briskly, out-of-doors, in every season. She's feisty. She's not afraid of being alone. Her face is lined and full of life. There's a ruddy flush to her cheeks and a bright curious look in her eye because she's still learning. Her husband often walks with her. They laugh a lot. She enjoys simple things. She likes to be with young people and she's a good listener. Her grandchildren love to tell her stories and to hear hers because she's got some really good ones that contain sweet, hidden lessons about life. She has a conscious set of values and the knack to make them compelling to her young friends.[1]

Jane Fonda wrote that in her best-selling *Woman Coming of Age*. Do I tackle life that enthusiastically? Or will my golden years be more like George Gray's, as described by poet Edgar Lee Masters:

George Gray

I have studied many times
The marble which was chiseled for me—
A boat with a furled sail at rest in a harbor.
In truth it pictures not my destination
But my life.
For love was offered me, and I shrank
    from its disillusionment;
Sorrow knocked at my door, but I was afraid;
Ambition called to me, but I dreaded the chances.
Yet all the while I hungered for meaning in my life.
And now I know that we must lift the sail
And catch the winds of destiny
Wherever they drive the boat.
To put meaning in one's life may end in madness.
But life without meaning is the torture
Of restlessness and vague desire—
It is a boat longing for the sea and yet afraid.[2]

What kind of old woman will I be? Feisty or frustrated? I'm laying the foundation now.

As Jane Fonda says, "Okay, Fonda, if that's how you want to see yourself at eighty, how are you going to make sure you get there? How are you going to live your life in your forties, fifties, sixties . . . ?

We do age. We wrinkle. We gray. Our bodies sag. Our lives burn out.

The crucial question then becomes: What am I burning out *for*? Where am I investing my limited energies? Which wounds am I choosing?

GETTING BURNED, FOSSILIZED, EATEN

Three word pictures have brought aging home to me: Life burns us. Life fossilizes us. Life eats us.

Life burns us. This is the thrust of a poem by T. S. Eliot. Yet, he continues, we have the choice of which fire we want—the fire of God, or the fires of our own selfish passions:

> The dove descending breaks the air
> with flame of incandescent terror
> of which the tongues declare
> the one discharge from sin and error
> the only hope, or else despair
> lies in the choice of pyre or pyre—
> to be redeemed from fire by fire.
>
> Who then devised the torment? Love.
> Love is the unfamiliar name
> behind the hands that wove
> the intolerable shirt of flame
> which human power cannot remove.
> We only live, only suspire,
> consumed by either fire or fire.[3]

Not burning up, but turning into fossils is the image drawn by writer Virginia Stem Owens. She describes how, as we serve people, they suck life from us. Mothers discover this quickly:

> Taking up a family is a good deal like consenting to become a fossil, itself a peculiar kind of earthen vessel. Fossils are made by the slow replacement of organic material with minerals. The hard structures of a living thing dissolve and are simultaneously replaced by other substances, pyrite or hermatic silica. The original organism has no control over the results. But the process does leave behind evidence of life forms for our contemplation. . . .

(Deciding whether to have children) comes down to a choice between accepting a certain porousness and insisting upon a definite impermeability. Between becoming a piece of limestone, through which life flows and filters, genes sluicing from the unalterable past into the uncontrollable millrace of the future—or becoming impenetrable chalcedony refusing imprint. A choice between the interstices of one's being clogged with the contingencies and consequences of other lives—or a polished, impervious self-containment.

Given a choice, God knows I too would have chosen the still, cold center of myself, safe from the flaws that the carelessness of others could inflict upon my surface. Aesthetically it certainly has more appeal. . . . Admitting other people into the process invariably means messiness. . . .

Fortunately, I wasn't given the chance to choose. Married at the last moment in history before women were widely supplied with that chemical barricade in the bloodstream, that contraceptive seine that strains out imprudent reproductive possibilities, I found myself at twenty-two with two strange interlopers in my life. The dissolution of my hard structures began. . . .[4]

"Eat or be eaten" is the world's motto, according to philosopher Loren Wilkinson, quoting Bertolt Brecht.[5] What is a Christian alternative? "Eat *and* be eaten," he suggests. That sounds revolting. It sounds cannibalistic. Yet we *do* take life from our mothers and from the sweat of the brow of our fathers. Incrementally, many people have given their lives to us. How can we repay them? By accepting their offering—and then giving our lives to others. We eat—and, in a sense, we are eaten.

WOUNDS: CHANNELS FOR BLESSING

Life wounds us. That is not the exception; that is the rule. We can't choose not to be wounded. We can only choose how we'll respond. Will we take these wounds as an affront, a surprise—or will we like Jacob wrestle to get the greatest blessing out of wounding circumstances?

Jacob limped forever after his struggle. We, too, bear the marks of our involvements. Including our involvement with time: We age. Yet often we can turn those wounds into channels for blessing others.

Josephine Butler is one woman who used her wounds to bless. Born in England in 1828, Josephine had loving and intelligent parents, beauty, a good education, a remarkably supportive husband, and four healthy children.

One evening Josephine and George, her husband, went out to dinner. When they got home, their only daughter, Eva, five years old, jumped out of bed and rushed out onto the upstairs landing to hug them. The stair bannisters gave way. Eva crashed to the tile floor below. George picked her up and rocked her. Her golden-chestnut hair hung bloodstained and tangled. Eva never regained consciousness.

Josephine and George each grieved silently. He took a new job so they could move to a new environment, and drowned himself in work. Josephine went out and hunted for an orphan who would look like Eva and took her in as a foster child. But she dreamed about Eva constantly—Eva running through the garden, Eva calling for her. Josephine prayed. She worked. She focused on her sons and her husband.

It wasn't enough.

One day Josephine confessed her restlessness to an old Quaker woman.

"Move out beyond your own sorrows," the old woman advised. "Go visit 'fallen women.' They need the pity and care you're lavishing on yourself."

Because Josephine acted on that advice, today she is world famous as a pioneer in helping prostitutes and poor women.

Many middle-class Christian women were involved in prison work. A movement among England's educated evangelicals had made social service fashionable. Like others,

Josephine brought food and clothes and tried to lead the women to God. But Josephine did more. She sat down with them and shared in their handwork. She listened. She touched them. She hugged. And she went with released prostitutes out the gates of the jail to the alleys which were their homes, where they had to find some means of support. She discovered the economic conditions which had pushed many into selling their emaciated bodies.

She opened a home for released prostitutes. Then the second Contagious Diseases Act was passed. It allowed police to grab any woman suspected of prostitution and subject her to a vaginal exam. It virtually ripped away *habeus corpus* for half the population.

Josephine exploded. She organized a Ladies Association which in turn published a well-reasoned protest against the Acts, signed by two thousand women, including Florence Nightingale and Harriet Martineau. She wrote books. All this was ignored by the government. So, reluctantly, Josephine took to the lecture trail (telling her mother-in-law that she was going off on "a sort of preaching tour of a delicate nature"!). In the first year, she attended 99 meetings and traveled 3,700 miles.

A strikingly attractive, stylish, well-bred woman, lecturing about pimps and surgical rape in an era of euphemisms when women were not supposed to know about sex, Josephine took a lot of abuse. So did her family. Her husband's career was derailed. Her sons, ages seventeen, fifteen, and twelve when she began, were the butt of jokes. Yet they stood behind her all the way.

Eventually the CD Acts were repealed. Then Josephine traveled internationally. She visited women in the immense St. Lazare prison in Paris, where she met five-year-old "prostitutes" confined to cages. Later, she and her family and friends, wearing disguises and using aliases, ferreted out facts about child prostitution in England. They actually bought a child, to show how it was done. The result was investigative reporting at its best. Josephine also lobbied against the sale of women to soldiers in distant India.

For twenty-five years Josephine never woke from sleep without seeing Eva crashing down and without hearing the sound of her head hitting the tile floor. But, following the old Quaker woman's advice, she used her pain as a stimulus to bless many others. As one of her biographers recorded, "She made all women who heard her care about what happened to some women."[6] If only we comfortable women today could be galvanized to care about poor women, instead of putting them in a box with the phrase, "They have a different lifestyle," and washing our hands of them.

Ayako Miura has also used her wounds to bless. She is a contemporary Christian Japanese novelist who has won a national prize for her work. One of her books, *Shiokari Pass*, has been made into a popular movie. Ayako Miura suffered from tuberculosis for thirteen years. During seven of those years she was in a body cast. Her fiance died of the disease. Through it all, Ayako Miura wrote. She also offered Christian witness to hundreds of other patients who visited her again and again in the room where she lay immobilized. Now cured, she is known for her patience and care in personal encounters, and for the theme, which appears in her works, of how Christian suffering can serve society. Through Ayako Miura's pain, non-Christian Japan has seen something of the beauty of Christ.[7]

Pandita Ramabai is another whose wounds became a stimulus for blessing. She was born in India in 1858. Her Brahmin father taught his wife and daughter Sanskrit, the sacred language which never was to be shared with a low caste person, or a woman. Ramabai grew up as a *Puranika*, a sacred storyteller. Her hunger for the sacred story led her eventually to Christ, to baptism, and to time in England and the U.S. Previously, the deaths of all her family except her infant daughter had led her to empathy with displaced Indian women. When she returned to India, she started a home for them. "Mukti"—"Salvation"—eventually sheltered 1,900 women at a time. Ramabai described it:

> The gardens and fields, the oil-press and dairy, the laundry and bakery, the making of plain Indian garments, caps, lace, buttons, ropes, brooms, and

baskets, the spinning of wool and cotton, the weaving of blankets, rugs, saris, and other cloths, embroidery and various sorts of fancy work, thread-winding, grain parching, tinning, culinary utensils, and dyeing furnish employment for hundreds of girls. Within the last few months, a printing press has been added to the establishment.[8]

Not only was "Mukti" practical. Revivals broke out. Many were baptized. Supporters both in the U.S. and India disapproved and withdrew funds. In this lonely abyss Ramabai took inspiration from Hudson Taylor and George Mueller: For the last twenty-five years of her life she ran her operation "by faith," rather than by guaranteed support. Such faith was nurtured by her Marathi Bible. She spent much time making a new translation of that.

Ramabai's hearers gave her the titles of Sarasvati—the Indian goddess of learning—and Pandita, teacher. She was the only Indian woman to have been so honored when Stephen Neill recorded her biography in 1934. But Ramabai did not rest in her learning. She asserted herself to create beauty and channel God's grace.

Pandita Ramabai. Ayako Miura. Josephine Butler. Three women who got hurt. Instead of shriveling up, though, they allowed their pain to make them more sensitive, more aware of needs. Their wounds became channels for blessing.

THE WOUNDED GOD

This shouldn't surprise us. Our God was wounded too. Yet out of his wounds healing for the nations has blossomed. Across the centuries people have been reborn through this paradox. Poet John Donne, writing in the 1600s, marveled at it. So did poet Luci Shaw, writing in the 1970s.

Donne mused:

Who sees God's face, that is self life, must die;
What a death were it then to see God die?
It made his own lieutenant, Nature, shrink,

It made his footstool crack, and the sun wink.
Could I behold those hands which span the poles,
And tune all spheres at once, pierced with those
holes?
Could I behold that endless height which is
Zenith to us, and our Antipodes,
Humbled below us? Or that blood which is
The seat of all our souls, if not of his,
Make dirt of dust, or that flesh which was worn
By God, for his apparel, ragged and torn?[9]

Three centuries later, Shaw wrote:

Blue homespun and the bend of my breast
keep warm this small hot naked star
fallen to my arms. (Rest . . .
you who have had so far
to come.) Now nearness satisfies
the body of God sweetly. Quiet he lies
whose vigor hurled
a universe. He sleeps
whose eyelids have not closed before.
His breath (so slight it seems
no breath at all) once ruffled the dark deeps
to sprout a world.
Charmed by doves' voices, the whisper of straw,
he dreams,
hearing no music from his other spheres.
Breath, mouth, ears, eyes
he is curtailed
who overflowed all skies
all years.
Older than eternity, now he
is new. Now native to earth as I am, nailed
to my poor planet, caught that I might be free,
blind in my womb to know my darkness ended,
brought to this birth
for me to be new-born,
and for him to see me mended,
I must see him torn.[10]

We like to be fit. We like to be in shape. But we age. And if we get involved with others, there is more cost. We bear the marks. Yet we follow the wounded healer. Sometimes, then, our very wounds can minister healing.

The summer my third child was born I had heavy professional responsibilities as well as three preschoolers underfoot. All of that I could manage. But overnight company I could not.

Yet, throughout the summer, several sets arrived.

About one woman I felt particularly bad. A gifted evangelist, a Ph.D., a young wife and mother, and a *friend*, she lived in a country tottering on the brink of revolution. She and her husband possibly were marked for extermination. Not surprisingly, that summer *she* herself tottered on the brink of nervous collapse. She came to visit. She needed attention. I couldn't give it. (Simultaneously I also had another family of four visiting!) After she left, I felt bad.

Later, when I went to my home office, I found a thank-you note from her on my desk.

Oh no, I groaned inside, another irrelevant note extolling me as Superwoman.

But no.

"Thank you for having me," she wrote. "You've helped me so much. From you I've learned that family life doesn't have to be perfect."

Our wounds can soothe others. To my friend, struggling to excel in so many areas at once, my imperfections ministered.

QUALITY OLD WOMEN ARE NEEDED

What kind of old woman will you be? What stretching experiences are you choosing now?

Quality old women are needed.

There's no college course on how to be a wife. So how is a bride supposed to learn to fill her new role?

"From the old women," says the Bible (Titus 2:3-4).

The old women? Those manipulating mothers and interfering mothers-in-law?

No, the Bible points out what kind of old women make good teachers. They're "not false accusers" (Titus 2:3). They don't gossip. Or stereotype a person. Or jump to conclusions. They're bighearted and broadminded. They know how to accept people who are different without judging them.

And they're "teachers of good things." They have something worthwhile to share because they've been involved with real life and have learned how to create beauty in it. Growing plants, making dishwashing a cheerful time for the family, or whatever—they can teach *something* authentically.

While we suffer from a poverty of cross-generation friendships, a young woman who will hunt for such an older woman is sure to be enriched. And a mature woman who is investing her life in something beautiful—and learning to guard her tongue—should never become unneeded.

What kind of old woman will you be? What fires are you choosing now? Let us choose the fires that will purify, the wounds that will soothe, the decay that will germinate life. Then we need not be ashamed when we die. Gardener Virginia Stem Owens muses in autumn:

> I look around me. . . . All is safely gathered in, and the rest, from the blighted squash to the bolted lettuce, leveled. I stand in the middle of my digging, surrounded by death. The breathtakingly beautiful golden-leaved cottonwoods glittering against the autumnal blue sky headed toward the winter solstice— they are only the ornaments of the death ship we sail on every year. . . . They console but do not distract from the fact of death. All about me the earth is dying, and I smile on it benignly. A decent decay settles over the earth. It is congruous: it fits all I know to be true about the world. It is not the obscene incongruity of a machine-gun suddenly splitting through the midst of a flowering plum thicket. . . . This is rather the death of Abraham, ending his life an old man.

173

My garden gets me ready for death. For if I, with that shadowy Adam at my elbow, live under the same curse he did, I have leisure to contemplate the death that will come to me. I see that it can come after a span of productivity, that it can occur with dignity. I shall not be ashamed to sift my molecules of matter into the succulent soil with the beans and corn as companions. God's curse always modulates into blessing.

But more than that, I shall become a voice in that great chorus of creation groaning in travail, in birth pangs, waiting through the long dark winter to be set free from decay, for "the redemption of our bodies" and the springing forth of the children of God.[11]

How should women live? What priorities should we choose? Esther was challenged: "Maybe you have come to the kingdom for such a time as this." Today we are supposed to pour out our energies for Christ and his kingdom, that his kingdom may come, that God's will may be done on earth as it is in heaven. Ask yourself: What have I come to the kingdom for? What dreams, friendships, and gifts do I have that are unique? What is not going to get done in this world unless I do it?

1. Jane Fonda, *Women Coming of Age* (New York: Simon and Schuster, 1984), pp. 14, 15.

2. Edgar Lee Masters, "George Gray," in *Adventures in American Literature* ed. Robert Pratt et al. (Boston: Houghton Mifflin Co., 1962), p. 276.

3. T. S. Eliot, "Little Gidding," in *Masters of British Literature*, Vol. II, ed. Rewey Inglis et. al. (New York: Harcourt, Brace and Co.), p. 1006.

4. Virginia Stem Owens, *A Feast of Families* (Grand Rapids, Mich.: Zondervan, 1983), pp. 98-99.

5. Loren Wilkinson, "A Christian Ecology of Death: Biblical Imagery and the Ecological Crisis," The 1975 Faculty Lecture, Seattle Pacific University, p. 1.

6. Margaret Forster, *Significant Sisters: The Grassroots of Active Feminism 1839-1939* (New York: Knopf, 1984), p. 201.

7. Ayako Miura, *The Wind is Howling* (Downers Grove, Ill.: Inter-Varsity Press, 1977).

8. Stephen Neill, *Builders of the Indian Church* (London: The Livingstone Press, 1934), pp. 181-2.

9. John Donne, "Good Friday 1613: Riding Westward," *Seventeenth Century Poetry: The Schools of Donne and Jonson*, ed. Hugh Kenner (New York: Holt, Rinehart, and Winston, 1964), p. 64.

10. Reprinted from *Listen To the Green* by Luci Shaw by permission of Harold Shaw Publishers, Box 567, Wheaton, IL 60189. Copyright © 1971 by Luci Shaw.

11. Virginia Stem Owens, "Go to the Garden Where Decay Redeems," *Christianity Today*, 17 December 1976, p. 346.

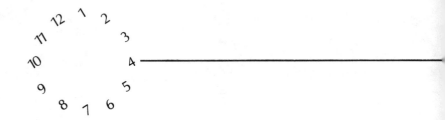

APPENDIX

Cultural Research Questions

GENERAL

Briefly describe the people's physical environment; demographic statistics; political environment.

FAMILY

1. What is the role of each member of the family?

2. How companionable is the husband/wife relationship? How much trust, respect, and understanding is there? How much disrespect, deception, or tension?

3. How much freedom does the woman have? How much authority? Give examples. How much education has she had? What is her ecomomic role?

4. How are the children taught? How are they disciplined? How important are other adults in socializing the child? How important is the child's peer group? How much does the father play with the child? How long do the parents control the child's choices? Is there a generation gap? How do people try to bridge it?

5. What do the old people do? How do other family members treat them?

6. How does the family make decisions? Who takes the lead? Is there discussion? How does the family settle quarrels? Describe some quarrels you have seen or have been told about. Who are the most loyal family members? Who are the least loyal? Are there some marginal members?

7. How is the family related to other structures in society: To the neighborhood? To kin? To community organizations?

SOCIAL

1. Who are the community opinion leaders? (These may include media and national as well as local figures.)

2. What is the community decision-making unit? What is the process?

3. How does the community settle quarrels?

4. What are the natural lines of affiliation? (These may tie individuals to several networks.)

5. In their most common group, what are the rights and obligations of members; any distinctive roles; special rituals or celebrations; myths or special reputation of the group; models; villains; other techniques of boundary maintenance; any distinctions between formal and informal behavior?

COMMUNICATION

1. What are their topics of conversation; joys; achievements (from their point of view); failures; heroes? What are they reading? Listening to? Where are they traveling? What questions are they asking?

2. Do they have any in-group language, codes, or symbols?

3. Do they have any distinct kinds of humor?

4. What kinds of media do they prefer: books, magazines, newspapers, leaflets, comics, radio, TV, tapes, drama, music, demonstrations, posters?

5. What style of verbal arrangement do they prefer: nonfiction, narrative, poetry, myth, proverbs, comics, debates; frankness or subtlety; abstractions or references to tangible things; induction or deduction; lectures or case studies; memorization or problem-centered learning; enthusiasm or formal presentations?

6. What are the main themes of columnists in national newspapers and magazines?

ECONOMY

1. What are the local natural resources?

2. What are the common local products made for home use or for sale?

3. What is the spread of occupations?

4. What percent are rich, comfortable, subsistence level, or destitute? Do these economic class lines coincide with other classifications (i.e., kin, caste, etc.) or do they cut across these divisions, tying people together?

5. What is the average daily diet?

6. Do they consider themselves impoverished, or not?

7. What kinds of expenditure do they delight in? (clothes, parties, insurance policies, investments, labor-saving gadgets . . .)

179

8. What kinds of expenditure do they consider extravagant?

9. What do economists think are the country's chief economic problems? Its assets? Its economic opportunities?

10. What do their neighbors think the country's chief economic problems are? How do they experience these?

11. Is there a Marxist movement among university students? What are their specific complaints?

12. Is there economic tension between ethnic groups?

13. What percent own their own land and/or business?

14. What are some of the most powerful political and economic entities in the environment of these people? How do they feel about these?

15. In the main, what social class in the national system do these people occupy? What are the functions or potential functions of this class in the total system?

16. How are large political and economic entities likely to affect these people over the next ten years? Hypothesize various alternative scenarios.

RELIGION

1. What do they turn to in a time of crisis?

2. What do they think is man's destiny? Man's origin?

3. What do they think will provide a full and meaningful life?

4. Do they think there is any transcendent power in the universe? Do they think they can relate to it? How?

5. What are their ideas of the supernatural? God? Christ? Man? Sin? Christians?

6. What moral system do they actually try to live by?

7. Do they participate in more than one religion? If so, when, where, and concerning what do they express each faith?

VALUES

1. What are their distinct felt needs?

2. What are their distinct values? (Contributing to needs/ values may be: economic problems; ethnic history; social tensions; marital or generational conflicts; problems in housing, schooling, medicine, legal justice; recreation; technology; childraising patterns; art; vocational aspirations; modernization or obsolescence; attitudinal emphases such as romantic love, loneliness, pleasure, family pride, friendliness, achievement, communal solidarity.)

3. What do these people consider to be the significant events of the last 30 years? Of the last 500 years? How have they reacted to these events?

SOCIAL EXTENSION NETWORK

1. What internal variations do these people exhibit: in language and dialect; in social class; in national citizenship; in geographic distribution, and in differing ecological milieus; in degree of modernization (including education, urbanization, types of jobs, desired family pattern and size, spending habits, etc.)?

2. What various networks tie members of this people to other people outside the group? What are the strongest externalizing networks?

3. Are a significant part of these people functioning customarily in terms of two (or more) cultural codes? Beyond the mother-tongue-and-culture, do the other codes come from: near neighboring peoples; early foreign colonizers/ immigrants who helped form the nation; recent foreign colonizers/traders?

4. Given multiple codes, do these people seem to evidence code integration or code switching? Is the code switching direct and cumulative? That is, are the people gradually changing from one ethnic identity to another over time? How do they feel about having multiple codes?

5. How do the people identify themselves? With what specific traits would they identify someone who is a member of their group?

6. How do their near neighbors identify them—i.e., with what specific traits?

7. How do they feel about their identity and ethnicity?

8. Is their ethnic affirmation maintained more because of a sense of satisfaction in their primordial roots, or because their ethnic identity gives them economic/political advantage?

9. If a church exists among this people, in what ways has Christianity enhanced their sense of their heritage?

10. In what ways has Christianity facilitated national integration? Has this eroded ethnic distinctives?

11. In what ways could Christianity enhance this people's ethnic distinctives?